The Disease of Government

H. S. FERNS

The Disease of Government

Maurice Temple Smith

First published in Great Britain 1978
by Maurice Temple Smith Ltd
37 Great Russell St, London WC1
© Henry S. Ferns 1978

ISBN 0 85117 165 6

Printed in Great Britain by
Billing & Sons Limited
Guildford, London and Worcester

Contents

For
M.

Preface

In 1944 Professor F. A. Hayek published a famous book, *The Road to Serfdom*. Professor Hayek's views were much discussed, often denounced and seldom or never attended to. Since the close of World War II the pace along the road to a collectivist society has quickened everywhere. The free, open and liberal society which men and women in western Europe began to envisage as a possibility in the eighteenth century and which seemed, during the nineteenth and part of the twentieth centuries, to be turning into a reality, is now fading away. Mankind seems to be returning to normal, i.e. to the condition observable during most of human history wherein the vast majority of individuals are locked in structures that they never made and cannot change.

Need this be so? It is the purpose of this book to explore this question. Can an individual make his or her life? Or, is the individual nothing more than a set of fingerprints with a number attached, and otherwise a problem managed and solved by someone else, some expert equally anonymous, managed and planned as himself or herself?

Society exists, but do individuals? Can they?

H. S. Ferns
University of Birmingham
January 1978

1 The Disease of Government

Most young people in the developed industrial world complete their formal education between their fifteenth and their twenty-third birthdays. In the Soviet Union and its satellite states the immediate future of the majority of these young people is assured. They will undertake compulsory military service. In the democratic states, on the other hand, their immediate future will not be so certain. Ten years ago—even five years ago—all young people at fifteen or sixteen years of age were sure of either jobs or opportunities for further education up to the level of their abilities. Today this is no longer so. The possibility—if not the probability—of unemployment faces young people just as it does older men and women regardless of their education and circumstances, or whether they live in the European Economic Community or the United States or Canada or Japan or Australia.

Unemployment today in mature industrial communities does not mean, as it does in the Third World, a total absence of income and dependence upon charity, scavenging or some other means of drawing sustenance from the surrounding society. Everywhere in the developed industrial world unemployed people can count on receiving money from the state. In Britain, for example, an unemployed person just out of school will receive £10.35 a week; a married couple £23.55 plus the rent of a house or flat. In some countries unemployment 'pay' is better, in others worse.

Whatever these payments to the unemployed are, they are

not magnificent sums of purchasing power. On the other hand, they are a means of living in poverty to which some at least can adjust as a way of life. When a community 'maintains' anything from 5 to 15 per cent of its working population unemployed, that community has within it a class of idle poor. When to the class of idle poor are added the probably more numerous but not easily countable number of persons drawing incomes in over-manned industries and administrative offices and in artificially created public employment, we are in the presence of a problem which even the most productive economy cannot safely neglect.

The cost to the productive part of the community is not at first the most important aspect of the problem. Unemployment or spurious employment in artificially created jobs engenders a sense of unreality and feelings of being frozen in a condition of dependence and helplessness which can only be improved by political action having either the humiliating character of begging and enlisting sympathy or the brutalizing character of threatening violence and social disorder. The consciousness of sharing and contributing, so important a constituent in social solidarity, is lost and in its place there develops either apathy or hatred. Thus by unemployment is society corrupted, and it is corruption on a massive scale.

The less immediate but in the long run the worst aspect of unemployment is the growing cost to the productive community. The conventional wisdom of the modern bureaucratic states, regardless of political colour, suggests two ways of 'curing' unemployment. The first is the cheap and economical method of paying the unemployed small sums of money for minimal maintenance like the £10.35 paid weekly to a 16-year-old British school-leaver. The other is the creation of jobs and the endowment of them with a 'purpose' such as 'modernizing' or administering or improving or providing goods and services which no one has ever asked for or supposed they needed.

Both methods cost the productive community something,

but the cost of the second method is vastly greater than the first. Both, however, have the long-run effect of impairing the productive power of the real producers in the community by reducing their capacity to maintain and improve their tools and organizational routines and by generating a strong sense of injustice among workers, managers and investors as the awareness grows that a substantial body of their fellow citizens are living off their efforts and intelligence.

It is now nearly half a century since massive unemployment emerged as a perceived problem in industrial societies. When it first developed in the great depression of the 1930s, in Europe and then in the United States and independent dominions of the British Crown overseas, the condition was corrected by the action of governments which culminated in World War II. This is not to argue that war was invented by governments to solve social problems—although the militarization of Germany by Hitler was a significant contribution to the process—but to suggest that war did in fact being unemployment to an end, and did provide the *modus operandi* of governments everywhere in the industrialized world to sustain high levels of economic activity and the employment and rising standards of living which this activity has made possible.

But now unemployment has returned everywhere in the developed world. No Iron Curtain marks the limits of unemployment and the misuse of manpower and resources. The only differences between the communist east and the capitalist west relate to the political and economic techniques used to conceal and deal with the phenomenon. A million men and women in an army are as much unemployed as a million men and women in receipt of unemployment 'benefits'. Both impoverish society and endanger its members.

If history were to repeat itself we should again go to war. This possibility cannot be excluded, but it is an eventuality so evidently suicidal that it cannot rationally be considered except as something absolutely to be avoided. Making jobs by piling up arms in the interest of a balance of power is no solution. Not only is this an extremely dangerous proceeding, but it is wasteful of manpower and resources and a tribute paid to fear, folly and paranoia expressed and rationalized in now-bankrupt myths and ideologies.

We have reached a state of development and crisis in which it is possible and necessary to look generally at what we have been doing to and with ourselves during the past half-century and at what may be the consequences for us of allowing the inertia of the past to control the future. Of the myths or rationalizations which sustain this inertia the most central and most pervasive is the myth concerning government. Government can do anything for us and to us and this is inevitably good. This is a form of faith as active and compelling in the United States of America, in Britain, in the Third World and in the EEC countries and Scandinavia as it is in the Soviet Union, its satellite states and in China.

A faith by itself is of no account in society unless it finds expression in institutions which instruct and control men and women. Faith in the state and in government is institutionalized in state bureaucracies constituted in varying mixes of civil servants, soldiers and political propagandists. What these bureaucracies do and can do to individuals and to mankind as a whole is now the question we must consider, for it is evident that these bureaucracies can no longer 'deliver the goods' in the shape of peace, order, and human well-being. Men and women cannot expect to create heaven on earth, but they need not create hell either. Indeed, on the evidence before us, the endeavour to create the first produces the second.

What above all seems to be our most important priority in our present circumstances is to create for ourselves a safe society. This need not mean a society free of hazards and disappointments for individuals or even whole communities, but one wherein the possibility is reduced of total calamity such as a nuclear war or the wasting of resources beyond our capacity to solve the problem of wastage.

Any argument which starts by calling attention to unemployment and then switches to the horror of nuclear war or the exhaustion of the world's natural resources seems at first sight to lack a sense of proportion. Unemployment is a comparatively minor evil compared with the destruction of peoples. But the connection is a real one. The bitterness and sense of injustice which unemployment generates not just in those unemployed but in those who have to bear the burden of paying for unemployment and jobs invented to provide incomes for those otherwise without work are the political constituents of the explosive mixture we call war.

Now that we have an adequate perspective on the past fifty years since our first encounter with mass unemployment, we can see that action by the bureaucratic state has not been an abiding or stable solution. The cost in lives and resources has been too great and the consequences in terms of civilized and satisfying life have been disappointing. It would seem, therefore, that rethinking is necessary.

Faith in government is faith, indeed: the substance of things hoped for; the evidence of things unseen. Let us then question the faith itself, and not its physical manifestations and their consequences in society. Let us suppose, for example, that government is not the doctor, but the disease. If this supposition has anything in it, the prescription we write ourselves will have to be changed.

2 The Problem

We have to start somewhere, and the place to do so is Britain. In any discussion of individual freedom, the rule of law, limited government and the participation of the subjects of government in political life, Britain is bound to command attention. From the early sixteenth century Britain has played a very considerable role in the characteristic developments of the modern world.

Today that modern world, insofar as it means the possibility for individuals of being potters rather than clay, is imperilled. This is particularly so in Britain where for three centuries the growth and development of personal liberty have gone hand in hand with increases in productive capacity, increases in knowledge, improved social cooperation and a more sensitive humanity. So long as Britain attracted the notice of the world on account of innovations in technology, increases in wealth, military power and expansion of enterprise and authority across the world, foreigners and Britishers alike associated the success of Britain with the political liberty which it was believed distinguished the British from other people around the world. Rebels against British authority from the American Sam Adams to the Indian Jawaharlal Nehru wanted only what the British were supposed already to have.

British conceptions of liberty were expressed in institutions and practices and not in what nowadays we would call ideologies. This had the advantage of allowing both foreigners and the British themselves to misunderstand what they were doing and to interpret the conception of liberty in a great variety of ways. It was possible within the British conception of liberty to build up an empire and to dissolve it; to develop the slave trade and to suppress it; to practise mercantilist control of commerce by the state, and to employ the power of the state to ensure a rigid and dogmatic system of *laissez-faire* in economic affairs; to leave the management of money and banking to the private ownership and judgment of individuals and private corporations and yet to insist upon and enforce the most exact and careful rules governing the issue of money and the giving of credit. The list is very long of what seemingly contradictory practices could be embarked upon by the freeborn British.

Although the liberty of the British was not susceptible to easy definition, there were some essential principles and practices underlying the laws and the actions of government, and it is the erosion of these principles and practices which is now far advanced. The elaborate technicality of the British legal system and the complexity of the political process in Britain are obstacles to seeing the essentials, and those well immersed in the technicalities of law and politics seem to be the least aware that there are principles of law and politics which can and should be stated and understood in language as simple and plain as that of the Constitution of the United States or the *Communist Manifesto*.

There is first of all the notion that each individual or combination of individuals, such as a family, a corporation or an association, possesses rights to do or not to do and duties which are obligations to do or to refrain from doing. These rights and duties provide a pattern of behaviour which enables men and women to live together, work together and cooperate with one another. If there are differences about the operational meaning of rights and duties, these can be resolved by third parties having no interest in the differences and capable of applying reason in assessing evidence and relating it to general principles.

This notion of rights, duties and disinterested inter-
pretation is very old in Britain and particularly in English
society. It was the organizing notion of the Common Law
and the Courts which were developed to establish peace and
justice. The notion is socially and morally valuable because it
recognizes that there are individuals who alone can
experience their own lives and feel their own joys and pains,
that there are also other people who are themselves
individuals and that there is an interdependence and an
exchange among individuals. The concept of rights and duties
residing in individuals excludes the possibility of judgments
being made by third parties except for the purpose of
resolving specific disputes about rights and duties.

If law is a matter of stating in a general form applicable to
all members of the community rules concerning the exercise
of rights and the performance of duties, the making, the
adjudication and the enforcement of the laws also involves
some underlying principles of structured action now often
forgotten or obscured by the complexity of the activity of
governing. The central conception as well as the practice of
the English Common Law required the presence of a third
party at once the judge and the enforcer of judgment should
an individual or a corporation seek to 'take the law into their
own hands'. Judgment and enforcement were indispensable
elements in making real rules of behaviour in society, but
neither the judges nor the royal agencies of enforcement were
themselves creators of law or controllers of society. Their
authority and powers of operation were limited to the specific
rights and duties under adjudication. On the other hand, they
were the creation of a monarch who was conceived of as the
protecting overlord and chief soldier. This he was so, in fact
as well as in conception. But the monarch was limited in his
role, for very good material reasons like poor communications
and the limited productive capacity of the community.

Historians like Stubbs who grew up in the age of
Victorian liberalism and *laissez-faire* believed that they could
discern in the ancient institutions of England the beginnings

of liberalism. There was some truth in this view. Government in medieval England *was* limited. There was a conception of open-ended rights and duties made operative by judges who defined them in relation to specific instances. Of course, there was much else in the medieval polity of England, but there was in it an element of flexibility which allowed something for individual initiative and social variety and worked towards the erosion of fixed status, towards legal equality of individuals and towards the organization of society in terms of contracts among individual and corporate bodies decided by the parties concerned and not by 'authorities'. It should occasion no surprise that serfdom, for example, had completely disappeared in England by the early seventeenth century, two centuries before this had happened everywhere in western Europe and two and a half centuries before it did in Russia. And it disappeared without any struggles specifically concerned with liberty, equality and fraternity.

In viewing the prospects of liberty in Britain today it is useful to reflect upon the more recent history of the country. Unfortunately such reflection is hampered by the technicalities and complexity of British history in much the same way that the principles underlying law and politics are obscured. In this matter our situation is much like that of Christians in the time of Erasmus when the complexities of theology and the canon law were obstacles rather than aids to faith in God and the appreciation of goodness. When the fifteenth was turning into the sixteenth century, Christians mouthed the words of their religion, but there were too many of them. So, too, perhaps, it is with us when we examine our history.

British historians today are divided roughly into two groups: the Marxists and the Eltonians. There are, of course, 'loose fish' swimming with one school or the other and uncertainly between the two. Both schools are seeking the truth, but for different reasons and naturally with different results. The Marxists are concerned with the future; the

Eltonians with the past; and neither very much with the present except as it relates to their personal professional or political fortunes. A third concern with history is, however, possible; viz. a consideration of the past as it reveals abiding and present dilemmas and problems, and the solutions thereof.

This third way suggests that political values, political behaviour and political institutions are inextricably bound up with the economic performance of the community, and that this in turn fixes the limits of, but does not determine the outcome of, political activity. Our forefathers made their own history; history did not make them. And so it is with us. History can only help in thinking about our situation.

So regarded, the history of Britain during the last half-millennium—roughly since the discovery of sea routes to the Indies and the Americas shifted the centre of the European world—suggests some situations and developments worthy of examination. The expansion of commercial communication from the confines of the Mediterranean and coastal waters of Europe to the coasts of Africa and the great oceans changed both the political circumstances and the economic opportunities of the nations of the British Isles. From being on the edge of the world they began to move into a central, or near-central position, and this attracted the attention and the enmity of nations richer and more powerful than they.

This change in circumstances began to come about almost simultaneously with the death throes of the military aristocracy, which had established itself in the eleventh century and had been one of the most powerful elements in the community for four centuries. Defeated and driven from the continent, the military caste had turned on one another in a long and bloody civil war. The victor, Henry Tudor, proceeded systematically to destroy the military, and to weaken the political and economic foundations of the aristocracy and at the same time to strengthen the finances, the administrative apparatus and the judicial authority of the Crown. He did this by the simple expedient of eschewing an expensive and profitless foreign policy, by good housekeeping, and by profiting from the confiscation and resale of the estates of his domestic enemies. Inasmuch as peace and public parsimony are always good for a community, the English benefited from what might be described as the politics of prudence.

This was not to last. His son Henry VIII bid farewell to all restraint in the matter of government expenditure. He inaugurated a regime, disastrously incompetent, extravagant, tyrannous, and often just foolish. The experience of the community at the hands of the Tudors was so terrible that it affected the consciousness of the English in every aspect of their life. It is not surprising that the greatest Englishman of that age should have made politics central to twenty-two of the thirty-seven plays which he wrote, and that Shakespeare's power of imagination and insight were so often addressed to the depiction of the activities of politicians: consuls, kings, queens, princes, courtiers and soldiers. The vast gallery of Shakespearean men and women of power is dominated by characters endowed with great energy and never contemptible, but, with the possible exception of one pure hero, Henry V, cursed in their lives, driven by ambition, jealous, mad, lustful, vain, confused, devious, cruel, murderous, vengeful, deluded and afflicted with hate. None of them had all of these characteristics, but one by one they were for the most part devilish combinations of vice and folly and their doom was more often than not death by violence. Compared with Shakespeare, no man has ever presented politicians in so fierce a light, and with such good reason.

But one mighty fact redeemed the Tudors. Elizabeth I preserved the national independence of the English, and saved the nation from becoming a colony of Spain, another Mexico. Without political independence the growing advantage of England as a commercial centre would have been lost to the English people. As it was, they were able to share directly in the benefits of the increased wealth which began to flow from the creation of a worldwide division of labour nourished with vast virgin resources of land, forests and minerals.

It is part of accepted wisdom to suppose that strong, efficient and responsive government is beneficial to communities. The experience of the English is otherwise. Strong, efficient government is the enemy of liberty and is of very limited utility to any community. This is well illustrated by the Tudor dynasty. In spite of a capacity for ruthless tyranny, brutal selfishness and cynical duplicity, or perhaps because of those qualities, none of the Tudors was able to solve the problem of making the Crown financially independent and of devising reliable means of skimming off the wealth of the community surplus to the basic needs of the people for food and shelter. In few communities in history have princes failed as the Tudors failed. The instances are not many: Switzerland, the Netherlands, Venice, some of the free cities of Germany, in some of the cities of ancient Greece, here and there, but never on a sufficient scale to alter a seemingly inevitable tendency in civilized societies towards exploitation of the creators of wealth by castes of non-producers. Armed with the means of violence, administrative capacity and priestly magic mixed in varying proportions, the castes of non-producers have over most of the world and most of history seized power and used it for their own purposes.

Unlike what was happening with too much success on the continent of Europe, where the Habsburg and Valois princes were struggling for absolute authority, the Tudor attempts at absolutism failed. Henry VIII, a wildly extravagant and cunning exhibitionist, ran through the resources accumulated by his father, and soon discovered that regal power of the kind he wished to practise demanded a steady flow of goods and services into his hands and those of his court. The devices for skimming off wealth were inadequate to his requirements. Too impatient and probably insufficiently practical, Henry resorted to the traditional expedients of cheating and robbery. He clipped the coinage and produced a roaring inflation and he seized part of the landed assets and a high proportion of the movable wealth of the Church. What he never succeeded in doing was to devise a rational system of taxation under his own control.

Robbery on any large scale requires accomplices, and these Henry was able to mobilize in ample numbers in the court and the Parliament. A sequence of events familiar enough to us developed. The Church, the principal object of Henry's rapacity, began to compromise, believing that by surrendering a little much might be saved. There soon appeared in the universities learned men inventing the most involved reasons to justify the crimes of the government.

Henry's mode of proceeding, however, had profound and unexpected consequences. Robbery differs from taxation in that it is a one-time operation. The most important part of the loot was a fixed asset, land, which could only be converted into revenue by devising an effective administrative apparatus designed to take the surpluses of production bit by bit and year by year. Henry's needs were too great and his demands were too exigent to be satisfied by such means. He was obliged to sell part of what he had stolen and to give away part to his supporters.

The fact of Henry's selling the land he had 'nationalized' depended on the existence of people who could buy. Why Henry did not rob these people—as Edward III had robbed the Jews—is hard to decide. Probably it was a simple matter of political arithmetic. There were more people with cash assets than there were churchmen in control of landed property, and it was easier and quicker to rob the Church and sell to productive people than to devise new means of taxing them. Whatever may have been the reasons for Henry's choice of selling assets rather than imposing taxes, the fact that he did so and the circumstances in which he did so can be seen now in the light of subsequent developments as an enormously important factor in the emergence of a new kind of economy.

Looking at the surface and considering the seizure and sale of a substantial part of the assets of the Church in isolation, it would appear that Henry had done nothing more than sell to men with surpluses of ready cash the right to collect the rent of land, much as the British government in 1977 sold its right to share in the profits of a large petroleum producer of which it was a part owner. More broadly considered, however, it had been demonstrated that the relationship between the men with cash assets and the government was an exchange relationship and not a subject relationship; that politically the merchants, landowners, butchers and bakers and candlestick-makers who had money or could raise money were in a very different position *vis-à-vis* the government than, say, the Jews had been *vis-à-vis* Edward III or the third estate *vis-à-vis* the King of France. Not only was the raw relationship different, but there was in the Parliament a legal and institutional means of dealing with the government. Because this was so there existed the possibility that money could fructify in the pockets of the people, and this possibility became an increasing reality as more and more opportunities came the way of the English on account of the expansion of the worldwide division of labour organized as commercial interchanges of the products of work.

From the reign of Henry VIII until a time within living memory a constant element in English and (since the Union of England and Scotland) British politics has been this relationship expressed in terms fundamentally of taxation between the government and the community. What proportion of the production of the community should be taken by the government? There were various thoughts on the subject, and a variety of expedients worked out, but the abiding concern of a large part of the community was to keep taxes low. Taxation was one of the questions which brought on the Civil War; not the size of the taxes, which were quite small, but the right of the government to levy them without the consent of Parliament. Attempts to spread the cost of government to colonies overseas precipitated the American Revolution. An increase of government expenditure from 11

per cent of the gross national product following the outbreak
of the wars of the French Revolution to 29 per cent at their
close produced serious and prolonged unrest. This steadily
abated as the proportion was brought down to 19 per cent in
1822, to 16 per cent in 1831, 11 per cent in 1841 and 9 per
in 1890.

This period of government expenditure declining in
proportion to the total production of the community was one
of economic success measured by almost any indicator one
cares to choose: population growth, production per capita,
intake of food per capita, house building, technological
innovation, saving and investment, improvements in literacy,
average length of life, etc. It was a period, too, when the
more sensitive spirits could begin to hope for the dissipation
of the darker part of the human heritage of cruelty, selfishness, bigotry and fear.

When we compare the Victorian experience with our own
we are bound to notice a serious change in the proportion of
the national production spent by the government. In the
centuries between the early Tudors and the reign of Edward
VII wars were the only government activity which seriously
altered the ratio of government expenditure to total production, and the normal tendency was towards a sharp
decline in public expenditure when the nation was at peace
with its neighbours. The Boer War increased the proportion
of the national product being spent by the government to 14
per cent, but even this modest figure declined to 13 per cent
in 1910, and this in spite of a large programme of naval
armaments and the inauguration of a state-supported welfare
system. World War I drove the proportion up to 52 per cent
in 1918.

After World War I the percentage began to decline again,
but it never again reached the low levels of late Victorian
times. In 1930 it was 26 per cent. In 1945 it was 66 per cent.
Under the Labour Government led by Attlee it was brought
down to 39 per cent. The Tories brought it down further to
37 per cent in 1955. This was the lowest percentage

achieved. Since then the percentage has risen no matter what party has been in office. It was 43 per cent in Macmillan's last year of office. It was 49.6 per cent in the last year of Wilson's second government, 1969-70. The Heath administration maintained the percentages of Wilson's administration, and as a result of the Tory 'reform' of local government administration, public health service administration and other measures having the effect of expanding the number of civil servants and the amounts paid to them, the percentage rose to 56.2 per cent in 1974 and is now up to 60 per cent of the gross national product.

Government expenditure of this magnitude is an indication that we have undergone a revolution. The outward signs of continuity—the Queen visiting the Commonwealth, the addition of new members to the House of Lords, the annual cycle of state rituals—mask a profound change in our socio-economic organization. We are in a mess because we have lost the power of making judgments about our own circumstances. It is a sad and humiliating fact that the policies of the British government today are not a product of the processes of British political life, but are a response to the judgment of an international body, the International Monetary Fund. It is something to do well because someone tells you to do so. It is better to do well because you yourself know what well is and have the self-discipline to do what you ought. That is freedom and liberty. Freedom and liberty are what the British community have lost. Why?

3 What is Government?

'Modern man' is a phrase frequently used to describe what we are. It implies that men and women today are different from their forebears; that being modern is at best desirable and at worst an inevitable fate. Japan has undergone a process of modernization successfully; Pakistan has not done so well, and Burma has not even tried. A few years ago the natives of Borneo were Stone Age men. Now they are modern men. The Egyptians, heirs of 4,000 years of civilization, have had 150 years of difficulty in modernizing themselves. Common to all engaged in this business of modernization, white, black, brown, yellow, red and mixed, is a belief in the magic of government. Government can do for men and women what, only two centuries ago, God alone could achieve.

The study of this sacred monster, government, occupies the attention of armies of learned men. The scholars and students peer down the trunk of the elephant, look up its anus, pull its ears, apply stethoscopes to its hide, describe the howdah, criticize the mahout and even cadge rides on its back. But few spare a thought for the poor peasants who supply the mountains of food the beast consumes. Even fewer ask the question, why elephants?

There are several ways of studying the monster. All of them yield information, but few yield understanding useful to the poor peasants collecting its food. The elephant has always been there; it will always be there, and the bigger it is the better it will be for all.

Thomas Hobbes, the English political philosopher, was a man too austere, logical and candid ever to command a popular following, but no man ever explained better the reason for the sovereign government's existence in relation to society. His explanation was based on assumptions concerning human nature: the natural propensity of each human being to maximize his or her power, which is the capacity to satisfy desires; the equality of all human beings; the fact that the satisfaction of all desires at the same time is impossible either on account of material scarcity such as the limited supply of natural resources or because of the contradictory nature of some desires (such as, for example, the desire for prestige). Human nature being what it is, the natural condition of man is a state of war, latent or actual. The escape from this condition of war is a social invention: the sovereign state. This invention consists in giving to one man or one institution an absolute monopoly of power on one condition: that peace be maintained and the natural condition of war prevented. The sovereign defines the terms on which individuals live with each other and expresses these definitions. What these definitions are do not matter as long as they are the means by which the sovereign achieves one purpose: the preservation of peace and order.

Like the authors of religious myths and parables before him and mathematical model builders after him, Hobbes' method of reasoning was to explore possibilities and consequences by stating what seemed to him irreducible, primal springs of human action whose management is necessary for individual and social life and for the continuity of human existence. By reasoning as he did, he came up with an analysis and recommendation which have an impressive record of acceptance, i.e. of translation of theory into practice. The sovereign state has replaced God as the definer of everything from the womb to the tomb. The only drawback to the sovereign state is the simple and massive fact that sovereign states have not brought peace to the world but a sword (nuclear tipped and capable of ensuring not eternal life but eternal death), and now sovereign governments threaten the lesser objectives of prosperity and economic security.

In the presence of our superabundance of theories about everything it would be a bold man who would say we need a new theory of the state. This we do not, but we need a new way (or rather the revival of some old ways) of thinking about government. The elephant of government need not be the star attraction in the circus. Once upon a time elephants did useful work in the teak forests of Burma, and probably still do.

Let us look at human nature and the state of nature. Except as a hypothesis the state of nature has never existed. As for human nature, let us agree that this is too difficult a subject for speculation. But this we do know. In the beginning there was work, and without work there was nothing. This is a simple, self-evident proposition, but somehow it commands little attention, and is the forgotten basis of economics.

Work is the expenditure of human energy both manual and mental for the supply of human needs. Needs, not wants. Wants can be foregone up to a point, and the point is where wants are needs. There may have been a time, and maybe there was once a place, where men and women picked their substance off trees as they appear to have done in the Garden of Eden. But there is not much evidence that anyone or any group of people capable of sustaining the continuity of life from generation to generation has ever been able to live without work. For the purpose of thinking about society this is a timeless universal fact. The Secretary of State of the United States consuming caviare at a banquet in the Kremlin, an Arab riding along a desert highway in a Rolls-Royce, a Treasury knight in a Rover, a drop-out scavenging crusts from a garbage can in Los Angeles and a beggar eating a handful of rice in Calcutta are all consuming the products of work. This seems an obvious fact, but it is not widely recognized. The activities of production and consumption are separate and any analysis which confuses production and consumption will inevitably lead to curious conclusions.

If the total production of a social group, no matter what its size, is only sufficient to meet the requirements of the group for food and protection from the natural elements, there is an equilibrium in the group with respect to consumption. If the equilibrium is disturbed from within, some will suffer and die; if the equilibrium is disturbed from outside, the same will happen. All must produce in order to live.

If, however, production increases significantly and the needs of food and protection from the elements are more than met by the total production, it follows that some of the community can live without work. All may, of course, be able to work less; all may equally consume more. But there is also a third possibility. Some can provide themselves with the means of life out of the production of the community by means other than productive work.

A bandit expends mental and physical energy in acquiring the means of life for himself, but he does not work productively. His relationship with society is to exchange nothing for something, and to achieve this by violence or the threat of violence. Equally a gang working a protection racket exchange nothing for something, but if there is more than one gang the victims can regard payments to one gang as a better bargain than exactions by two gangs. Once such a relationship develops, the gang which can guarantee peace and protection in return for regular payments is on the way to becoming a government.

There are certain general properties which tend to render stable over considerable periods of time the relationship between a government and its subjects. Banditry, protection rackets and governing are all specialized activities requiring their own expertise. And so is productive work. Specialists always in the long run triumph over amateurs in any line of endeavour. If one is a good farmer, a good miner or a good business executive it is not possible, except in the most extraordinary circumstances, and practically never simultaneously, for one to be good at government. And the reverse is true. Bandits, gangsters and princes are very seldom good at farming, mining and management. How often have we heard the cry, 'We need business men in government', and equally how often are business men dismal failures at governing. And how often are politicians failures as business men or farmers! It is almost an iron law of nature that governments are poor producers of goods and services, and workers poor governors.

Specialization of activity, whether producing or governing, is the most powerful reason why the community cannot get rid of government and likewise why it must have government. Producers require order and security in order to bring their activities to fruition. But the goods and services they produce can always be taken from them by specialists in appropriation. This is a fact of nature from which we cannot escape; or at least there is no evidence that any significant group has ever long escaped. The optimum solution for producers is to seek the protection which costs the least proportion of the goods and services produced, but an optimum solution is difficult to achieve, and very seldom has been.

So far as we can judge from the material artefacts which have survived from the ancient civilizations of the Mediterranean and Middle East, the resources of manpower over and above those needed to provide food and protection from the elements were used by the political controllers of those societies for the prestige and adornment of themselves and for the administrative and military apparatus which were their instruments of power and their means of extracting income from producers.

The most impressive of these civilizations in terms of size and administrative sophistication was the Roman Empire. Initially a republic of farmers armed to protect themselves and their main productive resource, land, the Romans

developed a formidable military apparatus the use of which
yielded greater returns than the work of farming. The
Romans, therefore, developed the arts of appropriation which
they carried to such a peak of perfection that in the end the
apparatus of the government collapsed and the empire shrank
from a political jurisdiction embracing western Europe, the
Middle East and North Africa to the city of Constantinople
and some dependent territories of varying size. The remains
of Roman fun and games, the great arenas and baths, and of
their administrative and military apparatus, their roads,
harbours and fortifications are very impressive evidence of
how they used their manpower. The basic activity of the
subjects of the Roman Empire was the production of food,
clothing and shelter, employing tools and techniques of great
antiquity. This production nourished what the political
masters of the Empire prescribed or found necessary for the
preservation of their power. The workers on the land
provided the means of sustaining miners, stonemasons,
soldiers, administrators, craftsmen producing armaments and
consumer goods for the city dwellers and the mobs in the
cities who shared the imperial exactions and lived on
subsidized food and enjoyed publicly financed baths and
entertainment. The Roman government was a popular
welfare state of consumers living off the work of others.

The exploitive nature of the Roman government had a
powerful influence on the character of the economy and the
development of productive technology. Architecture and civil
engineering flourished and applied chemistry produced
innovations like cement which hardened under water. The
Roman roads were unequalled in scale, accuracy of surveying
and solid construction until the age of railways. Their
purpose was military and administrative convenience, and yet
those who moved over them walked, rode horses or moved in
carts drawn by oxen. The improvement in efficiency of
transport relative to the expenditure of manpower employed
in their construction was very slight. Six hundred years after
the Romans left Britain, soldiers moved from the borders of

Scotland to the English Channel along prehistoric trails just as fast as Roman legions had moved along Roman roads, and probably just as fast as ancient Britons had done 600 years before the Romans arrived. The point is that, impressive as they are technically, the Roman roads were *not* of much significance in terms of production.

Another ancient empire of vast dimensions was the Chinese. It, too, exhibited the characteristic features of a society wherein the arts of control and the appropriation of surpluses were developed and refined. The Chinese dynasties developed much more stable structures than the Romans, and these endured for nearly three millennia. The dynasties changed, but the system remained. The Chinese were a vastly ingenious people of many skills and high intelligence, but little of this was translated into better tools and greater production. The structure of power ensured that nothing would happen to disturb a finely balanced system by which a government and its supporters lived off the people who worked and produced.

The empires of antiquity, some of them not so long ago brought down, suggest, if they do not conclusively prove, that government as such contributes very little to the production of goods and services. All governments cost something, and the cost of government is always a subtraction from total production. But there is a legitimate question: is the cost of government a necessary social cost which must be borne by the producers, just as an industrial firm may have to bear the cost of the road system which makes industrial production possible? The answer is: yes and no.

The Roman government seems to have contributed very little to the productive effort of the community. The *pax romana* was worth something, but the cost of government was enormous. The cities of the Roman Empire were centres of consumption. As such they generated a great variety of productive activities, for example, the building of complicated and marvellous water supply systems, the arts and crafts devoted to the adornment of public buildings and private residences and so on. But anything which we would describe as capital investment designed to cut the ratio of human effort to goods and services produced and to expand production was largely absent. The productive effort of ancient civilizations was manpower-intensive and remained so. There were certain advantages to be derived from a geographically extensive division of labour, but even this important element in economic development was diminished in effect by the exploitive nature of Roman government. The flow of commodities to Rome, for example, was not in the main an exchange of goods and services between Rome and, for example, the North African provinces, but a despatch of tribute: the one-way traffic which is characteristic of the exactions of the politically powerful from the politically weak. Profits were, of course, made by merchants handling the corn trade between Rome and North Africa, but these were not profits on a productive investment flowing into a pool of spending power used to provide for depreciation and to finance further production. Out of profits Roman corn factors might finance more ships or even the expansion of the area of production and the purchase of slaves, but the total and cumulative effect of Roman exploitation of the grain lands of North Africa was to exhaust them and turn them into deserts.

The effects of government on the Chinese economy were not essentially different from those in the Roman world, but the Chinese, having in very distant times expanded to natural frontiers everywhere except in the south, developed a long-term policy of equilibrium so much part of the imperial mode of behaviour that it was hardly a policy but rather a philosophy of life encapsulated in the writings of Confucius. The military aspect of government was much less important in China than in Rome. The hierarchical nature of society was deeply rooted in the consciousness of the people so that there existed concepts of 'good government' by just emperors and of 'bad government' by corrupt officials. Bad government manifested itself as increased exactions and arbitrary behaviour, when the distinction between banditry and government became blurred. Then the secret societies began to form. Rebellion broke out, like that in recent times by the Tai Pings and Boxers, the corrupt dynasty was overthrown, and a new pure government installed. But the system did not change.

What part the Chinese emperors played in production is not at all clear. In some areas of China great irrigation works were the result of government effort and supervision, and these were obviously an important contribution to the productive system. Bad government meant not only arbitrary and increased exactions, but administrative failures, and thus political revolt could have a productive dimension as well as being a resistance to exploitation beyond well-established norms. None the less, political action against the government in ancient China and down to the revolution of 1911 did not seek changes of structure and purpose but the restoration of the norms which distinguish government from banditry and give exploitation of producers the character of ordered civilization.

Both theoretical speculation and historical evidence suggest that there is a natural tendency in human affairs to move towards the achievement of a state of equilibrium in which producers accept what they cannot avoid, i.e. the appropriation of surpluses of production for the maintenance of a minority who consume but do not produce. This equilibrium is static and tends to preserve technology at constant levels or at levels of very low rates of change. Observation and ingenuity satisfy curiosity, command admiration, and demonstrate human capacity but they do not lead to changed methods of production. The spirit and capacity of man tends to express itself in art and not in utilities.

Experience during the past two and a half centuries has cast doubt upon the notion of a static equilibrium between producers and exploiters as an inescapable social norm. Fixing dates for this experience exposes the fixer to easily made criticism at the hands of historians with precise but restricted knowledge. In spite of this difficulty, it is a big fact that human society at least in western Europe began to exhibit some novel tendencies during the eighteenth century, and that these tendencies have spread and intensified so that almost any measure we care to apply suggests that the condition of man in the last quarter of the twentieth century is vastly different from that of man in the seventeenth century. How was the static equilibrium broken, which for millennia manifested itself as a norm to which societies tended to return? Is there any explanation for the emergence of societies in which the surpluses of production were canalized into the purchase and use of more and more productive tools and more and more complex divisions of labour and not into the production of pyramids, baths, gardens, administrative structures, cathedrals, palaces and ceremonials? Why did a concept of individual freedom emerge, and why was the fact of status diminished? Why did the practice of exchange become a predominant mode of human relationships instead of remaining a practice of pariahs and lower castes?

Let us suppose ourselves engaged in the business of prophecy in, say, the middle years of the fifth century AD. Prophecy is usually the projection into the future of past experience. This being so, we could prophesy that the Roman Empire, now shrinking beyond recognition, would rise again, or that something very similar to the Roman Empire would take its place, bringing together into one divine agency of God or the gods the several races and nations of men from south to north and east to west so that deserts to the south, arctic forests to the north, the great ocean to the west and the mountains, spaces and the empires of the east would set the true boundaries of the world. Here there would be built again the peace and order which legitimize government and distinguish it from banditry and barbarism.

Such a prophecy made in the fifth century AD., we can see now, would have been wrong. It has not come to pass, but not for want of trying to restore or replace the Roman

Empire. The term Holy Roman Empire only disappeared finally as a possible political concept at the beginning of the nineteenth century, and for at least a thousand years the construction of such an empire endowed with a solid material reality was a not unreasonable goal of a variety of politicians, soldiers, and priests. And yet it never did happen, and the more one looks at the record one can see that it never could have happened.

What did develop in Europe was a force more all-transforming than any Caesar ever conceived of or could possibly have conceived of. What has happened to the world in the last five hundred years has been the work of Europeans. As matters stood in 1939, when World War II broke out, Europeans controlled the whole of the African continent, a substantial part of the Asiatic continent, and the Middle East. European settlers controlled the Australian continent, the islands of the Pacific from large islands like New Zealand to the smallest atolls. The most powerful state in the world, the United States of America, was a product of European enterprise and settlement. What the Americans did not control in the Americas was in the hands of European settlers: the British and French in Canada, Newfoundland and the Caribbean; the Spaniards and Portuguese in Latin America.

The only exception to white, European power around the world was the empire of Japan. Somehow the Japanese had managed to do something which even the enormous, ancient civilization of China had been unable to accomplish, i.e. to learn from the European some of the politico-economic essentials of 'modern life' and to apply them for their own participation in the business of empire building.

The impact of the Europeans upon the rest of the world is customarily discussed in terms of imperialism. The word itself tends, and sometimes is intended, to associate the politics of European expansion with the archetypes of ancient empire and particularly the Roman Empire. But the expansion of Europe, which had achieved its ultimate political expression by 1939, differed fundamentally from the expansion of the Roman Empire.

At the heart of the expansion of Europe were improvements in productive techniques, and these improvements were not primarily or principally in weapons or military organization, which are the instruments for the extraction of wealth by political means. The great European empires of the Far East, those of the Portuguese, the Dutch and the English, were not established by conquest, and the wealth they yielded came from trade. The Europeans fought with one another, and India became a British sphere of influence and eventually a possession through British victory over the French. The British control of India by military power took place *after* they had established themselves as traders. At the very end of British rule in India there were vestiges of their first *modus operandi* in the East, namely areas ruled by Indian princes with whom the British had made political treaties which involved the Indian princes trading their power for the British protection of their right to extract the produce of the labour of their subjects as their predecessors had done for centuries and even millennia. But the main activity of the British from first to last was economic: to expand and secure opportunities first for trade and then for the investment of capital. The British transformed India, converted a vast subcontinent from an antique society based on agriculture into a modern industrial society knit together internally by railways and connected with the great world by shipping lines and commercial organization.

Not all European expansion overseas followed this pattern. The Spanish Empire developed from the early sixteenth century along Roman lines. Mexico and Peru were conquered. The governments of those societies were utterly destroyed. A centralized administration was set up. The Crown of Spain extracted from the Americas what it valued most and needed most: precious metals. All else was subordinated to the mining of silver. Trade and industry developed, but they did not flourish either overseas in Mexico and Peru or in Spain itself. Once the imperial system was fully established, as it was by the 1560s, and once its real purpose came into operation, the existing transformation of Spain in consequence of its vast expansion gave way first to a pause in Spain, then to stagnation and then to positive decline of population, industry, trade and power. The endeavour to create a new Roman Empire failed.

This is not to say that the Spanish Empire in the Americas did not endure long or longer than other European empires overseas and did not have an impact upon the peoples subject to it similar to that of the Romans upon the barbarians they conquered. The Spanish Empire failed as the Roman Empire failed, and as the other European efforts at expansion did not, because it was not a factor in the breakthrough of a European metropolitan nation to new levels of human capacity manifest in technology, capital accumulation (which is a generalized way of indicating an increase in the quantity and quality of productive tools), increased economic interchanges and population growth.

Contemplation of the failure of the Spanish Empire takes us to the heart of the question: why did man in western Europe break through the barriers fixed in the ancient world by the dominance of a consuming elite over a mass of workers, and move on to new conceptions and new proofs of man's capacity to master nature, to use its resources and powers and to show new evidence of man's share in the creative force which was once attributed only to God Himself? Why was it that man has been able to reveal some material evidence of the notion foreshadowed in the Christian doctrine of the Trinity that men and women contain within themselves some of the power of God?

Man, like God, moves in a mysterious way his wonders to perform, but this is no obstacle to enquiry and speculation about what he does and has done. Why did the revival of the Roman Empire or a structure similar to it never take place? The myth and the intention were there for a millennium and a half. A possible brief answer is this, and it is a political one.

Government as an agency of consumer interests after the manner of the ancient empires was never able fully to reassert itself in European society. Governments of a kind there always were everywhere but, from Charlemagne to Napoleon to Hitler, the construction of a 'thousand-year Reich' was never possible, though often dreamed of and sometimes attempted. The fact that governments were numerous and various imported a flexibility to society with some important consequences. Slavery, for instance, diminished and in parts of Europe disappeared entirely. Thus the harshest, most exploitive and most long-standing control of producers by consumers was attenuated and never revived in Europe.

The idea and the institutions of a sole authority in and over society were undermined and for a very long time were inoperative. The Emperor who is God disappeared, and the allegiance of men and women became dual or multiple. The idea and the fact of a spiritual community, the Church, provided a large new element of social flexibility, and some of the institutions of the Church provided an opportunity for the development of large-scale organizations of producers such as monastic orders, e.g. the Benedictines. In orders of this kind the whole product, or nearly the whole product of labour, was retained by the productive community and some of it was reinvested in the improvement of productive techniques for the glory of God and as evidence of the capacity of man to improve and develop the capacity to work, to exploit unused or under-used resources and to provide examples for the larger society. The temptation existed in the Church for its professional leaders to become a consumer interest, a problem never solved and which in the end produced revolt. The fact that it produced revolt was itself a matter of immense significance.

Of great importance, too, was the emergence in European society of communities whose governments were the instruments of producers themselves. The Venetian Republic, the city of Genoa, the free cities of Germany, the independent cantons and cities of Switzerland were communities of workers organized by merchants, and sometimes by craftsmen. It is a common illusion of modern currency and of great antiquity that merchants are exploiters of workers. Yes and no. Merchants differ from soldiers and government administrators in that they are themselves an organizing part of productive processes and that their way to wealth and prosperity depends upon the exchange of goods and services and not upon their extraction from producers. They may seek to skim off a maximum proportion of the produce of labour for themselves, but they can only convert themselves into pure parasites by joining the consuming elite as landlords, or bureaucrats or politician/soldiers. While individual merchants may be able to do this, like a Medici, or a Gladstone or a Kennedy, merchants as a class cannot. Making a profit is only possible as a part of creative productive activity.

During the millennium following the collapse of the Roman Empire in the west, Europe was able to resist and escape the imposition of imperial control by first the Arabs and then the Turks. The resistance to the prospect of Oriental despotism was decentralized, and the resistance did not lead to the creation of a counter-despotism controlling all of Europe. Indeed, the assaults of the Turks on the Holy Roman Empire of Charles V were utilized as an opportunity on the part of a great variety of European authorities to wreck any plan the Habsburg family may have had to convert the Holy Roman Empire into a real Roman Empire. Power in Europe was so diffused, and its socio-economic foundations so various and so strong, that a centralized, armed and rationally administered political system was impossible.

Considered as a whole, the political system of Europe was a competitive one in the sixth century as much as in the twentieth. Competition for resources, for prestige and for power and all the advantages which power is supposed to

bring imparted to society a dynamic character. Through the
Dark and Middle Ages Europe witnessed development in
depth and breadth never known under the authority of
Rome. The Italians never flourished so greatly nor contributed so brilliantly to the development of human skill as
they did from the thirteenth to the seventeenth centuries
when, as a community as distinct from a state, they suffered
from no yoke of a general government.

It was argued that the chaos of the Italian political
condition was a great weakness. Machiavelli, for example,
looked back to the Roman Empire as an alternative to a
polity which allowed larger and more consistently organized
political forces from France and Spain to ravage and
dominate the Italian lands. He taught a doctrine which
aimed at the creation of a single strong, secular authority
drawing on the full resources of manpower and wealth to
create a unified political community. This was an attractive
solution of the problem of political competition, and the
construction of stronger, better-organized governments
became the objective of princes and kings and of almost
anyone capable of a general view. What can be worse than
anarchy and war? The question is still with us.

One consequence of political competition in Europe is both
massive and obvious. Struggles for power which never
produced a victory for one force or combination of forces
were a stimulus to development, economic, technological and
intellectual. There is hardly a feature of modern science and
technology not attributable to wars both hot and cold, and it
is equally the case that the great progress of mining and
practical metalworking in Europe from the tenth to the
seventeenth centuries is explicable chiefly by the demand for
weapons and armour. The stable hierarchical empire of
China was the community in which chemical explosives were
most developed, but there they were a curiosity and a source
of exciting entertainment. In Europe these chemical
explosives were put to military uses and so was set in train a
succession of developments which today manifest themselves

in nuclear knowledge and the adaptation of high-energy physics to lethal use in political struggles.

Little wonder that the imperial officials, having sampled some of the knowledge and a few of the less benign aspects of European civilization, decided to close the doors of China to European intrusion at the beginning of the nineteenth century. Even less surprising is the fact that they failed. There is indeed something devilish about Europeans, particularly when looked at by peoples living in communities which, even today, do not possess their knowledge and their techniques of using it.

Considered from another angle, it may be argued that the European competitive political system, taken at any point of its history, did not involve a distribution of the products of work substantially more advantageous to producers than obtained in the empires of antiquity or in the contemporary Oriental despotisms. The European workers worked, the soldiers, politicians and administrators consumed the surpluses in accordance with the 'natural pattern' postulated. But there was a substantial difference in the consequences.

The fact of political competition imposed upon the most active competitors the need to improve their armaments, and this conditioned the development in the communities they controlled. They were obliged to create either the industries which provided their arms or economic activities which enabled them to buy arms from other communities, and were sometimes obliged even to buy men as well as weapons. The strong interest in the supposed wealth of the Indies seemed to the princes and politicians of the sixteenth century to be a means of supplying themselves without having to make any politically dangerous concessions to workers and merchants.

The Emperor Charles V was especially successful in this regard, and his son Philip II of Spain followed in his footsteps. With what consequences? The bullion taken in Mexico and Peru and the silver-mining industries established there were used to nourish the political enterprise of endeavouring to dominate Europe. At first the effect was to invigorate the economies of Spain and western Europe, but soon the policies first of the Emperor and then of the King of Castile and Aragon began to exceed the productive capacities of the communities they controlled. Money was borrowed on a great scale and the population had imposed on it the heavy burden of inflation. The economy of Spain was so debilitated that by comparison with the rest of Europe Spain became a backward nation whose population declined during the seventeenth and eighteenth centuries, and it remained a backward, semi-colonial area until the 1960s. The attempt to establish a new Roman Empire that was something more than a name failed miserably.

Every effort by politician/soldiers to establish political control of Europe came to grief as the Spanish Habsburgs did. The French tried it twice and failed both times. So did the Germans. Each endeavour stimulated the economy initially; then financial disorder followed, manifesting itself as inflation and/or debt repudiation; then came political revolution, either generated from within or imposed from without. Unlike the Spanish case, the stimulus to the French and German economies flowing from the efforts of the politicians to triumph in the contest for continental power did not lead to economic degeneracy. The tools and the skills were not lost, and in both the French and German cases it required only a revolutionary change in political leadership for fresh efforts at European hegemony to be made: Napoleon after the French Revolution and Hitler after the overthrow of the Kaiser.

The most significant breakthrough in the direction of a free, open capitalist society developed in communities on the margin of continental European politics: in Britain and in the United Netherlands. The political elites of those communities never aspired to the control of Europe. Their political posture was always defensive, and their active participation in the politics of Europe had always the object of preventing the dominance of the continent by a single political authority. Their comparatively small size, their location on the edge of Europe, and their closeness by sea to the Americas, the coasts of Africa and the Far East engendered in the British and the Dutch a similarity of response to opportunities. They were not immune from the costs of competitive politics as regards either their own rivalry or their joint endeavours to prevent the domination of Europe by the French monarchy. In fact the cost of competitive politics to Britain and the Netherlands involved expenditures of unprecedented size for both states.

But they had compensating advantages which enabled them to bear this burden, to prosper and to develop their productive capacity all at the same time. Once their independence was assured by the defeat and exhaustion of Spain, the way was open for the English, the Dutch and, after the Union, the Scots, to take advantage of their maritime position to expand to worldwide dimensions the division of labour which was then, as it still is, a major factor in increased productivity. This they were able to do at very low cost in terms of public expenditure. English and Dutch expansion was not by way of military operations financed by taxation at home and looting abroad, but chiefly by way of trade and colonization, activities which depended on the mobilization of private surpluses, the development of methods of investment, and the management of productive processes and commercial operations.

Although the Dutch paid some attention to colonization in areas of low population density in North America and Brazil, their main effort was directed to trade in the populous parts of the Far East, particularly in the East Indies. The effort of the British was more wide-ranging and various, a fact easily explicable in terms of population. The population of the British Isles was greater than that of the Netherlands, and that population was wracked by political and social tensions which served as an incentive for emigration.

The significant breakthrough to a free, expansive, capitalist economy came in British North America. The planting of new communities overseas was inevitably a filtration process. Some of the old society of the mother countries was taken overseas, but much also was left behind. Particularly significant was the great importance in the colonizing process of the predominant presence of working, organizing and trading elements and the comparatively small and unimportant place of the vested interests of parasitic consumers associated with government and landholding. The place of government, aristocracy and military and ecclesiastical organization was much diminished, so that at any point in the history of the British colonies in North America, even after revolution had liberated thirteen of them from their mother country, the communities there were very different from anything which existed in Europe.

The first big fact about North America was its vast size, the richness of its resources of land, building materials and river systems of communications, which in the first stage of development could be used at little or no cost.

And this treasure house, unlike Mexico and Peru, was almost empty of people. The Indians were stone-age men scattered in tribes who lived by hunting and food gathering. They had little that white men could steal and they were for the most part mobile forest dwellers who were hard to catch and hard to convert into labourers either by enslavement or by the payment of wages. On the other hand, the Indians of North America were very generally quick to recognize the advantages of trade. Iron cooking pots, iron and steel tools such as axes and knives, blankets and guns greatly improved their productive powers, and they quickly discovered that the European would exchange these for furs and herbs, which they knew how to produce and which for some reason inexplicable to them the white men valued more than they did themselves. The law of comparative advantage began to operate almost from the first contact with Europeans, and white explorers were often amazed to discover that Indians who had never seen a white man used products of European industry which they had acquired by means of trade well before they had encountered people from overseas. So long as there was no conflict over the use of resources, the colonists, the European merchants and the Indians lived in a cooperative relationship with one another. In the territories of the Hudson's Bay Company a stable, peaceful relationship between Indians and Europeans lasted for nearly two centuries, and the only violence there was that of Europeans fighting Europeans for opportunities to trade.

The abundance of land and resources and the scarcity of people profoundly influenced the character of the society which developed rapidly along the seaboards and up the valleys of the rivers flowing into the Atlantic Ocean. Any economic development anywhere and at any time requires financial resources to provide the means of life and the tools for workers during the several stages of the project from its conception in the mind of an entrepreneur through to the production of a commodity which can be used by someone, somewhere, and for which the consumer will pay sufficient at least to cover the cost of production. Those who possessed purchasing power, or were able to obtain it from others with surpluses over and above their requirements, were key people in the process of development. But money without people is nothing. The recruitment of a labour force was, therefore, essential.

The political economy of labour recruitment is not easy to describe. Land and resources were abundant and were therefore cheap compared with land and resources in Europe. Furthermore, the vast spaces to be occupied made it very difficult to exercise socio-economic controls designed to keep down the price of labour. The attractions of savagery were considerable to Europeans and, like Huck Finn, not a few Europeans were inclined 'to light out for the territories' when they found that they could not abide the discipline of settled society. Controlling the frontier and fixing it as a limit beyond which Europeans could not go was an impossible task, and one which in the end helped to bring on the American Revolution when the British government attempted to carry it out. In Europe men and women could and did become vagabonds and criminals as an alternative to labouring and producing, but there no real alternative existed to working for others either as an obligation of one's status or as a means of earning a wage. In North America there was room for an alternative, and of this purchasers of labour power had to take account.

The combination of abundant resources, the difficulty of imposing socio-economic controls and the relative scarcity of labour were the foundation of a new kind of society constituted predominantly of free individuals subject to little control by government and bound together socially by contractual relationships expressed principally as the exchange of goods and services with each other. The patterns of learned behaviour, which made the practice of free contract and of buying and selling possible, derived mainly from religion and from traditions of social cooperation developed in Europe. Even in the matter of religion the importance of established organizations staffed by professionals controlled from afar was much diminished in the British colonies. Religious experience was more a matter of individual enlightenment derived at first or second hand from the Bible, which is itself a repository of the social experience, the spiritual insights and the knowledge of God gained by Jews and Christians, both minorities outside or opposed to the great power structures of the ancient world.

The predominance of exchange relationships in the British colonies, when applied to the recruitment of labour, had diverse results. At first those men of means in England who were resolved for a variety of reasons to emigrate to America organized, as John Winthrop did, the transfer to the New World of as much as possible of their own community in England. But it was soon found that the circumstances of America relaxed or dissolved the hierarchical relationships of old England, and that labour was most easily recruited by buying the obligation of individuals to work for a term of years in return for transportation to America. The supply of labour was further increased by the practice of the authorities in Britain of commuting sentences on vagabonds and criminals to transportation to America. In effect, British social problems were exported to America, and insofar as absence of economic opportunities was the cause of the problems this was a rough but not unintelligent or necessarily inhumane solution. Taken all together, these methods of labour recruitment made it possible for some match to be made in America between economic rewards determined in favourable market conditions and the combination of physical energy, mental awareness and luck which are the natural determinants of the individual's place in society. It is not at all surprising that by the time of the American Revolution more popular wellbeing was to be observed in the North American colonies of Britain than in Britain itself.

But there was also a dark side to labour recruitment by trading methods. It was discovered on the west coast of Africa that labourers could be bought as slaves. The contract of purchase was not with the individual but with the owner of the individual, and the obligation to labour was not for a term of years but for life and for the life of the progeny of slaves for ever. The colour of the labourers identified them, and their cultural and tribal heterogeneity ensured that they could not combine to achieve their individual freedom. The subjective nature of the white men's religion enabled them to rationalize the enslavement of the blacks, and their self-interest caused them to degrade the slaves to the equivalent of cattle and to devise for their control methods of rational management that were applied to cattle.

The effect upon Europe of rapid development in America was profound. The British community began steadily and rapidly to grow during the eighteenth century, and the wealth of the community became such that more and more was available to improve the tools, the communications systems and the overall productive powers of the society. At the same time it enabled the British to engage successfully in the competitive politics of Europe, not to seek domination but

to drive European rivals out of the overseas trading opportunities. The Seven Years War was the first truly world war,
and the British won that war partly by their own military
and naval efforts and partly by financing allies on the
continent of Europe.

In so doing they created a great crisis for themselves.
Which way? Towards the construction of a vast apparatus of
government capable of controlling the frontiers of America,
governing India and policing the oceans of the world; or to
face an absolutely new set of circumstances in a profoundly
new way. The instinct and the interest of men in government
is always to enlarge their power and authority. This manifested itself in the government of George III as a determination to tax the American colonies, to force them to pay
for the cost of driving the French from North America, and
to sustain the military power necessary for empire on a world
scale.

The American colonists rightly saw in this a threat to all
that had been done in America to create a new kind of
society. Much could be said on behalf of the British in terms
of ordered, hierarchical civilization and traditional conceptions of justice, but very little could be said for them in
terms of economic development and personal, individual
freedom, at least for white men. And the British at this stage
had nothing to say on behalf of black men.

Debate and passive resistance turned into war. The
absolute monarchy of France thought that by befriending the
rebellious colonists and giving them military assistance it
could undo French defeats around the world. Once again the
competitive politics of Europe contributed to the breakdown
of ordered hierarchy and brought to birth new forms of
society. The assistance of France swung the balance in favour
of the American revolutionaries. The British themselves,
beginning to doubt the wisdom of overmuch government,
quickly gave up, and even more quickly recognized the
independence of the United States of America.

At the time this was regarded as little more than an

incident in the competitive politics of Europe. With the benefit of hindsight we can see now that the American Revolution was one of the turning-points of history. There was born then a possibility of government of the people, by the people and for the people. The idea of self-government was apprehended and discussed and so emerged from books into the public consciousness. This happened among a body of people numerous enough to have some significance in the large world. These people lived in a land rich in resources. They lived, too, sufficiently remote from the main centres of hierarchical civilizations, beyond the effective reach of their power and authority. The American Revolution was a real and significant break with ancient civilization and equally with the modifications of ancient despotisms made by Europeans during the thirteen centuries between the collapse of the Roman Empire in the west and the day when a Boston mob threw the East India Company's tea in the harbour and challenged the British government to see who ruled.

In his speech at Gettysburg, eighty-odd years after the establishment of American independence, President Lincoln recognized the contingent nature of government of the people, by the people and for the people. Without effort, this possibility can perish from the earth. Without this recognition of contingency, Lincoln's words are mere sentimental rhetoric. Man makes himself, but into what? Is the experience of man in America but a brief aberration in history, a discordant note in the music of time, or a new kind of music for everyone?

4 The Foundations of Freedom

Writing in England in the atmosphere of Victorian optimism, the jurist Sir Henry Maine observed that 'the movement of the progressive societies has hitherto been a movement from status to contract'. He shared the widespread belief derived from immediate experience that human-history is a record of progress susceptible to intelligible definition. His studies of ancient law and his experience of government in India suggested to him that the most general thing we can say about progress in legal and political terms concerns the transition from the fixed social categories of ancient societies to the uncategorized individuality expressed in social arrangements established by consciously made or consciously accepted agreements among equals. To a man of Maine's experience in India, status was an active fact of social and economic life much more than it was in England, and as a man who on the whole considered progress both inevitable and desirable he expected the thrust of policy and legislation to be directed to the production both in India and in Britain of societies in which equal rights and duties would belong to everyone.

There are many difficulties about the concepts of status and contract, but they do provide a convenient means of discussing freedom as a social condition. The concept of status implies inequality of rights and duties among members of a community bound together in some way, usually by an authority having power over the community sufficient to enforce the inequalities. Contract, on the other hand, implies social, political and economic intercourse arising out of agreements among individuals or groups of individuals to do or not to do defined things.

It is a manifestation of status if an hereditary right enables certain individuals to sit in the House of Lords or in another society obliges men to undertake only certain kinds of work. Before the American Civil War, a slave in South Carolina might perform the same tasks as a farm hand in Ohio, and he might be better fed and better housed than the farm hand, but the slave had a fixed social position defined by the laws of South Carolina whereas the farm hand had the right to work or not work and for whomsoever he wished that belonged equally to all other citizens of Ohio. This was a real and well understood difference which had nothing to do with the question of whether the slave ate more protein than the farm hand, had more square feet of floor space in his dwelling and could count on food, clothing and care in his old age. Freedom is actually better than slavery on any reckoning, and it would be difficult to find anyone anywhere who would argue otherwise.

Slavery is quite well understood, at least in the abstract, but is freedom?

Freedom and liberty are widely approved words. What do they imply? What social, economic and political relations are required for individuals to be free?

We can accept the proposition that a man or woman can be spiritually free in any set of circumstances.

> Stone walls do not a prison make
> Nor iron bars a cage ...
> If I have freedom in my love,
> And in my soul am free;

and Solzhenitsyn's Ivan Denisovich demonstrated his free spirit by surviving for another day in a labour camp. True. But the possibility of spiritual freedom does not require us to accept that individuals are free in a society in which one body of men and women can define the truth, and operate an

administrative apparatus which identifies individuals who do
not accept truth so defined or are otherwise deemed objectionable, and which then compulsorily prescribes the conditions
of life and death of those individuals. No one would seriously
argue that England was a free society when governed by a
Parliament which ordered the cropping of a man's ears
because he had claimed for himself some of the characteristics
of Jesus Christ. It would be equally difficult to argue that the
United States was a free society when a man could be tarred
and feathered for crying 'God save the King!' or lynched on
the strength of a rumour that someone had raped a white
girl. It is quite easy to state the circumstances, legal and
social, in which individual freedom is non-existent or limited.
It is likewise very difficult to describe any set of circumstances in which all individuals are free in the sense of
being able at all times and in all places to do or not do
anything they wish.

Put in the most general way, one can say that an
individual is free in those circumstances wherein he or she
has the opportunity to do or not do what is necessary to
ensure his or her life. Inasmuch as the indispensable
necessity of all is to work, it would seem to follow that
freedom requires circumstances in which individuals may
work and thereby live. As we have already observed, the fact
of working exposes the individual to the possibility of having
taken from him all or part of the produce of work. To the
extent that this happens the freedom of the working
individual is reduced.

It is evident from experience that the productivity of work
is increased by the division of labour, the improvement of
tools and the development of sustained patterns of social
cooperation. If for the moment we leave aside the robbery
problem, which is the origin of government, we must
consider the possibilities of individual freedom in complex
systems of production. In any productive system the fact of
the division of labour dictates that all participants in the
system do not do identical work. How can the rewards of

work accruing to individual participants in a complex process of production be determined, if all contributions to production are not the same?

The same natural possibilities exist in a productive system as there are in society at large. All participants necessarily cannot have equal knowledge of the system or equal skill in operating the system. This is not necessarily a matter of difference in intelligence, character and energy, although these factors may have some bearing on the matter. Each participant has so much time and energy, and these can within wide limits be used only in specific tasks. A skilled mechanic is not a skilled manager and a skilled manager is not necessarily a skilled financier, i.e. a man or woman skilled at assembling resources from the surrounding society required to sustain current costs. A skilled mechanic may be transformed into a manager or into a financier, but necessarily he or she cannot perform the same functions simultaneously in any productive system of an elaborate and complex character. The possibility, therefore, exists as a natural fact that distribution of the rewards of work will not correspond to inputs of energy, intelligence and creative effort, and that one group of specialists will take out of the productive system more than they put in. If government becomes involved in productive systems the possibility of one group of specialists exploiting another group of specialists is greatly enhanced, and the problem of achieving justice in a productive system is thereby diminished. At least this would seem to be what experience suggests.

But the problem of distributing the rewards of work among the participants in a productive system is not simple. Production results in utilities—goods and/or services. These are measurable in some way, but even when measured how are they to be shared? How can we determine whether a skilled mechanic gets x per cent of the end product, a financier y per cent and a manager z per cent?

The problem is not made simpler by measuring the goods and/or services produced in terms of money. At one time this might have helped, but money, one of man's oldest social inventions, has been so abused by governments that neither in time nor in space is it any longer a good measure of value or a store thereof. But in any case our concern is with real goods and services and how they can be divided and by what social mechanisms or practices.

The whole problem is beset by a host of delusions. One of the most common is the notion that the sum total of goods and/or services can be divided in accordance with some principle of social justice. We know from experience that individuals have in varying degrees a sense of justice, and they will be satisfied if they think justice is being done to them or their friends or more generally to everyone. Contrariwise they will be discontented and even rebellious to the point of violence if they think that injustice is being done to themselves and sometimes to others. But the operative words here are 'if they think'.

We can agree that satisfaction will be maximized in proportion to the degree to which individuals think justice is being done in the matter of distributing goods and services. The question is 'how can maximum satisfaction be achieved in the matter of justice?', and this is very much a matter of how the results of a distribution are achieved.

This is where freedom comes in. Participants in a system of production know that they contribute something to the activity, and they expect to get something out of the activity, be it planting a garden, designing a bathing suit, teaching a child to write, or welding on an assembly line. Their activity is intended to provide for their natural necessities and their felt wants. They do something for others and they expect others to do something for them. The relationship is an exchange: a two-way relationship. One cannot exist without the other.

A sense of justice or satisfaction or acceptance in this two-way relationship is engendered by two elements, firstly a consciousness of doing something or creating something oneself and secondly a consciousness that the reward for so doing is the best one could achieve having regard for the overall circumstances in which the effort is made. Justice, satisfaction or acceptance are feelings and thus the springs of action or potential action (for feelings can be suppressed or accumulated as resentment), but feelings themselves are generated by physical facts and experience. Any productive system which relies heavily upon the manipulation of feelings unrelated to the real, physical experience of participants is bound to be unstable. That is why stable systems of production rely upon the existence of alternative opportunities for the participants. If the participant does not regard as fair or sufficient the exchange of his or her effort or assets for rewards, he or she can seek an alternative so that the upper level of rewards can be discovered. Once that upper level is known, the participant knows that justice is being done or that one must be satisfied or must accept the rate for the job, or the rate of profit on savings or the return from the sale or rent of an asset. Justice, satisfaction or acceptance are socially generated, but it does not follow that justice can be determined by anyone but the participants themselves on the basis of their experience as producers.

The incomes of participants in a complex system of production are acquired in three ways: by exchanging labour power, i.e. the expenditure of energy both physical and mental in producing goods and/or services for money, which is a general claim on all goods and/or services; secondly, by exchanging purchasing power not used immediately for consumption goods and/or services for a percentage share in future production; and thirdly, by exchanging the use of an asset such as land or physical resources for purchasing power.

Participants in a productive system have, thus, three categories of reward which the old political economists of the eighteenth and early nineteenth centuries called wages of labour, profits on capital and rent of land. In modern economics the category 'rent' has disappeared, largely because the cost of land and resources has been merged with the cost of capital generally as far as the accounts of enterprises are concerned. From the point of view of anyone saving out of income, savings can be used to purchase land and resources in order to acquire a deferred income in just the same way as one can purchase capital claims for the same purpose.

Yet one can see why the early political economists attached great importance to rent. Thinking and writing at a time when modern enterprise was emerging, men like Ricardo regarded labour and capital—workers and tools—as the active elements in the productive system. Land, on the other hand, was an essential, but the owners of land could acquire an income by renting or selling this essential without contributing anything to production. The Dukes of Northumberland, for example, owned large estates beneath the surface of which there were deposits of coal. Colliery operators organizing production and providing tools and miners working in the pits were obliged to provide a large income for the Dukes of Northumberland in the shape of rents for the right to mine coal. The Dukes of Northumberland did no work, except the work involved in organizing a rent system for ensuring the family an income. They contributed nothing to production as such, any more than the owner of a building site in New York or Hong Kong contributes to production in return for contracting either by sale or by renting to allow others to use a space he has not created or produced, but of which he can claim the ownership.

Politicians, soldiers, priests, and other non-productive elements in society have always recognized the importance of rent as a means of acquiring a share of the end products of labour. In the empire created in the New World, the Crown of Spain never allowed anyone to own outright the land or resources of Mexico and Peru. They rented these assets or charged a toll on production. The modern oil sheikhs, or the Shah of Iran, the politicians who govern Venezuela and the controllers of other OPEC countries have contributed little or nothing to the production of petroleum in their countries. But they have learned how to collect a rent for these operations. They seek to legitimize what they do in a variety of ways, but the fact that they are air-conditioning deserts, or attempting to become great military powers, or promoting revolution or ending poverty serves only to obscure the fact that they and their revenues derive from ownership and control and not from work in its many forms.

Rent as an income extracted from productive workers by the owners of space and/or resources has something in common with taxation in that it is a deduction from the output of the productive. Rent may be, but is not necessarily, returned to the productive system as an investment for increasing or improving the stock of productive tools or increasing the incomes of producers. The great English landlords of seventeenth- and eighteenth-century England will serve to illustrate this point. In 1790 there were some 400 of them and their incomes averaged £10,000 a year. They owned 20–25 per cent of the cultivated land. They spent their revenues in a variety of ways, mainly on consumption goods: some on palaces and parks; on the products of skilled craftsmen and artists; on sport; on travel; on education and learning; and some on the improvement of the tools, organization and resources of agriculture and industry. This last kind of expenditure was an addition to the stock of productive capital and hence a return of rent to the productive system. There is much evidence that the English landlords as a whole did help to finance agriculture and industry and were to that extent contributors to the development of several important parts of the productive system, and a source of investment funds necessary for the financing of increasingly complicated industrial processes and commercial infrastructure such as canals and roads.

If we accept that total production will not be shared by all the producers and that a proportion will be paid to owners of space and/or resources for their use, we can then consider how the remainder is distributed to the participants in production. It is obvious that in any productive cycle, i.e. from the production of the raw materials to the placing of the finished product in the hands of the consumer in exchange for money, there is bound to be a period of time during which the ongoing requirements of the participants in production must be satisfied. Furthermore it is obvious that tools are required in production and that these tools themselves are becoming increasingly costly as technology and 'tool effectiveness' develop. It follows from these practical facts that there can never be a distribution of the total product of the productive cycle to the participants which they use as the means of purchasing consumer goods and services. The total wages and salaries of producers, no matter how calculated, can never equal or surpass the value of the end products no matter how calculated. If they either equal or surpass this value, tools will wear out, improvement in tools and organization will cease and production will fall. This will happen no matter what name is given to the productive system: capitalist, cooperative, socialist, communist or anarchist. This is the sense in which it can be said that economics teaches one essential truth: there ain't no free lunch.

The problem for any society is, therefore, how to devise methods of dividing total production between that part devoted to the financing of tools, organization, stocks of raw materials and components of production and that part available for consumption by the participants in production. This can be done in a variety of ways, and experience seems to suggest that some ways are better than others and some do not work at all.

The method to which the name capitalism or free enterprise is applied is based upon the notion, expressed in customs, laws and institutions, that individuals are the owners of themselves: i.e. their power and capacity to work and the products of their work. This ownership and control means freedom of use, i.e. absence of constraint by others in the disposition of the products of work either by consuming them, leaving them idle or exchanging them for other products of work, either goods or services. The assumption is that each individual is governed by self-interest. Self-interest is an open-ended concept inasmuch as it has no objective definition, no necessary consistency in individuals, or in a collection of individuals or over time. In the matter, however, of supplying one's own needs, self-interest is simply a disposition or a tendency present in nearly all human beings to do what will satisfy wants.

Working, producing and exchanging the products of work in accordance with self-interest is a form of social cooperation, the consequence of which is a division of labour, of specialization of skills and of increased production. As a barter system, it has serious limitations because surpluses over and above current needs are inflexible and, being in a physical form, are subject to deterioration. The use of money makes it possible to accumulate surpluses in a more flexible and universal form. Money, of course, is a very ancient human invention, and its functioning did not necessarily lead to capitalist forms of economic organization. Indeed, money as a form of wealth presents an advantage to bandits, soldiers, governments and non-producers generally.

None the less, the existence of money as a means of social cooperation was indispensable to the emergence of a capitalist economic order. It is in no way surprising that the most extreme anti-capitalist romantics, such as Fidel Castro, see the abolition of money as a means of inaugurating an alternative society. Money makes possible the accumulation of surpluses of purchasing power.

A mere accumulation of money, however, is not capital. Money becomes capital when a set of circumstances obtain wherein significant sums can be used on a sufficiently large scale and in a persistent and continuing way to organize production, purchase tools required and sustain long production cycles necessary in any complex division of labour. These circumstances began to obtain in parts of Europe and most importantly in North America in the seventeenth and eighteenth centuries. Not for the first time in history, but for the first time on a large enough scale, accumulation of purchasing power surplus to current needs of consumption could be devoted almost exclusively to the purchase of the only source of production, viz. labour. The proportion of the surpluses taken by governments and rentiers was, for reasons already stated, small by past standards, and the main thrust was in the direction of buying labour power to make more money in an ongoing process.

A feature of a capitalist system which distinguishes it from ancient and medieval economies and from socialist and communist systems is the existence of a specialized group, the entrepreneurs and financiers who can only exist by maintaining and developing a system of production. They must accumulate capital and invest it. This was not true of the soldiers, politicians and priests of the medieval world. When Lenin and his colleagues seized power in Russia in 1917 they inaugurated a command economy which they called war communism, but once the emergency of war had passed and they wished to repair the damage they and their enemies had done and to get the Russian economy moving once more, they reintroduced a capitalist system, which they called ironically the 'New Economic Policy'. When Stalin abandoned Lenin's policy in order to inaugurate a system of socialist planning, he was obliged to resort to force, the institutional manifestation of which was a vast system of labour camps. These camps had two well-defined purposes: (1) to turn labour into capital or products like gold and timber which could be exchanged in the capitalist world for capital equipment; and (2) to terrorize the 'free' workers, peasants and intellectuals and to render them malleable, controllable and conformist. The brutal alternative to the generation of capital by saving, investment and the use of the free labour market is something that has been insufficiently considered or even acknowledged by contemporary socialists, but it is quite easy to understand why trade unionists as different as those who supported the Republican Party in the

United States and the Labour Party in Britain in the 1920s and 1930s were anti-communist. A free labour market is *free*, whatever else may be wrong with it.

The fact is that a capitalist system has built into it as a condition of its existence the need to produce goods and services and nothing else. Individual capitalists may seek to convert themselves into gentlemen and rentiers and play at being feudal potentates, but even when they do so their assets remain in the system and their incomes depend upon the profitability of their investments, which in turn depend upon the production of goods and services. No one but a fool could suppose that a Duke of Marlborough ever married a Vanderbilt because the Vanderbilts had ceased to be capitalists, or that Hearst ceased to be one because he imported a feudal castle into California.

Because a capitalist system is based upon exchanges, of labour power for wages, of investment funds for rights to share in profits and of goods and services for goods and services, there is a complex opposition of interests among the participants in the system. While it is a useful first generalization to say that there is an opposition of capitalists to workers, this does not get us very far in analysing the network of interests which interact in the system. The notion that workers and capitalists are homogeneous social groups in opposition to each other is quite wrong. They cannot get along without each other, if for no other reason than that exchange relationships are at least two-party relationships which cannot exist in separation. Put in the crudest way, capitalists cannot exist without workers, and workers cannot work without capitalists. But, 'Ah, yes,' say the socialists, 'they can.' Not and be free, is the answer.

Economic freedom or free enterprise denotes a set of circumstances in which the participants in the process of production are able to decide for themselves whether and on what terms they will exchange an asset, be it the capacity to work or a sum of purchasing power, or a portion of space and/or resources for another asset which they need or want, be it a wage or salary, a share in profit, a sum of interest or any other object of their need or want. This freedom is not an absolute freedom. It is contingent upon there being at least two parties to the transaction and that there is a two-way flow of satisfactions.

Economic freedom also requires a set of circumstances in which there are alternative possibilities for the parties to the exchanges; circumstances in which the rates of exchange—so much butter for so much tea—are determined by the parties being able to discover by comparison the exchange which yields the maximum of satisfaction on both sides.

The circumstances in which exchanges can take place resulting in the maximizing of satisfactions are not natural or inevitable in society. Their creation depends on the absence of a disposition on the part of any of the participants to effect exchanges by violence so that the flow of satisfactions is one-way, and the choice is between your money or your life; or to effect exchange by fraud or misrepresentation, or by the application of techniques of psychological aggression. It may be said that a system of free exchanges can be worked effectively only by a parliament of angels. And this is so in the sense that a system of free exchanges requires the development in the participants of honesty, love, and regard for other human beings, in short of a sense of the necessity of doing as ye would be done by. It is not accidental that Quakers, for example, have been successful business people because they attach importance in their lives to the qualities of honesty and love, and are, therefore, trustworthy and so capable of creating relationships which have some stability and continuity.

These qualities of honesty and love are quite consistent with hard bargaining. An honest and loving man or woman is not a softy, nor is he or she required to forget his or her own interest and the desire to maximize his or her satisfactions. What is required is a recognition that maximizing one's own satisfactions requires the maximizing of the satisfactions of others. This is most possible in circumstances where there are alternatives in exchanges; where the worker is not compelled to work for any one employer; where the employer is not obliged to employ any particular worker; where the possessor of capital is not obliged to invest in any one particular project and where the owner of space and/or resources is not obliged to sell to any one purchaser. In these circumstances the parties to exchange are not obliged to consult their consciences in making an exchange, but are able to do the best for themselves that the overall circumstances permit.

Who can say what is the rate of exchange of a barrel of petroleum for a quantity of butter? No one can, but society or an aggregation of individuals can; provided all who need or want butter and all who need or want petroleum have the opportunity freely to express themselves by stating the price they are willing and able to pay. We know very well that this process of exchanging can be perverted or corrupted or disorganized by the intrusion of political methods backed by violence or the threat of violence, but the fact remains that no individual or group can say what the rate of exchange of commodities and/or services should be. They can decree what is, and they often do so, but the extent to which they do is the extent to which they destroy individual and collective freedom and deny people the power to control and make their own lives.

An economic order organized as a system of free exchanges has a number of merits long ago recognized but now forgotten or obscured by cant. The first of these is the creative tension and discipline which individual self-interest balanced against individual self-interest imports to the economic order as a whole. A worker who knows that he will lose his opportunity to work if he does not fulfil the terms of his contract of employment, and that he will be replaced by one who will make an honest exchange of labour for wages, is under the same discipline as the employer who knows that he will lose the services of employees if he does not pay the same wages as his competitors and maintain the same conditions of work. The social solidarity, social peace and productivity observable in communities where these conditions are most nearly met is compelling evidence of the advantages of a free exchange system. Where these principles of economic organization have been most nearly met, in the United States of America, in Great Britain between 1840 and 1914 and in some of the overseas communities established by British initiatives in the eighteenth and nineteenth centuries, there was a degree of social peace and solidarity which contradicts the massive generalizations about class antagonism and revolutionary struggle. It is state intervention in the economies of these communities and the growth of myths about abstract social justice that have produced and are producing class struggle, and not the systems based on free exchanges.

The second merit of a free exchange system is the provision it makes for the creative imagination which resides in individuals and the opportunity it affords for this creative power to be translated into real utilities which people are willing to avail themselves of and to the production of which they are willing to contribute through exchanging their assets for such utilities.

The third merit of an exchange system grows out of the responsibility which necessarily rests on the individual to provide for his or her own life as a whole. The free individual must provide for himself or herself the economic resources for the whole of life from childhood to death. In systems which provide for the sustenance of individuals from the womb to the tomb, the individual never grows up and never matures except sexually. Life is a perpetual childhood, and the life of a spoiled child at that. The sense of material reality is lost and the thrill of testing oneself and displaying one's abilities is reserved for sportsmen, artists and entertainers. For the people at large the experience of life becomes a second-hand spectator activity. Work itself becomes routinized boredom, instead of what it can be, the centre of one's life and its exciting necessity.

Arguments which depend for their force upon a promise of material abundance are bound to attract the contempt and even the ridicule of those who are already provided for, such as, for example, the millions in western Europe and America who are neither immensely rich nor cramped in poverty. The satisfactions which material abundance brings are limited, and men and women can be bored even more easily by abundance than by its opposite.

It is at this point that the moral and political aspects of capitalist society need to be considered lest the precious jewel of freedom and individuality be cast in the mud and lost perhaps for ever. Men and women can be robbed of their personalities just as they can be robbed of the fruits of their work. This is particularly true of those whose principal property consists of their skill and their power to work. That is why all men and women, no matter what form their property may take—whether labour, capital or resources—require the existence in the human consciousness of concepts of rights and duties. On those concepts can then be founded the intellectual and moral principles which inform the structure and working of the institutions of society. Because no man or woman can live alone, rights and duties are inextricably bound together and are not separable without the destruction of society or individuality or both.

We know from history and from present observation that societies have been and are constituted upon the principle of an unequal distribution of rights and duties, and that a great variety of arguments can be adduced to justify such a distribution. In the presence of these possibilities the believer in the worth and significance of individual freedom must be a believer indeed and a dogmatic one.

This faith and this dogma consist in the assertion that society is made by and out of individuals and not the other way round. The individual comes first, because it is only the individual who experiences life, who knows the satisfactions and bitterness of living and who works and creates, physically, mentally and biologically. Individuals give and receive, and not social aggregates. It is arrogance to suppose that one man or one woman or one group of men and women can know what is good for another or for a collection of others, and it is a high crime against humanity to act upon such an assumption.

Individuality is a natural fact. Any system of morals which supposes otherwise is either a catalogue of errors or a means of rationalizing the devices by which some rob others either of their property or of their personalities.

The Christian injunction to love God and to love your neighbour as yourself is a sufficient foundation for a system of morals provided always that care is taken to give equal weight to all that is contained within the injunction. Firstly there is the vast power of the universe outside oneself, creative, largely unknown but not unknowable and of which we are a part. Secondly there is the power of knowing and acting which belongs to the individual. Thirdly there are the others like oneself whom one is enjoined to respect and consider in the way one does oneself.

These propositions seem self-evident, but individuals do not grasp them naturally and involuntarily in the way that they learn how to breathe or blink their eyes. They have to be learned and understood. Moreover, they have to be translated into customs, social practices and institutions so that they become operative in society.

Individual freedom is an open-ended concept only up to a point. Freedom does not mean that 'anything goes'. Political, social and economic freedom are no different in principle from the freedom a natural scientist has, and must have, in the presence of the universe which he or she is investigating; that is to say, the scientist is not seeking a foregone conclusion which he can borrow or make up for himself, nor can the scientist make up any kind of test of truth or relevance of what he does; nor is the scientist free of the necessity of learning the techniques of observation and analysis required to investigate the objects of study. And yet a scientist enjoys, and must enjoy, the freedom which consists of an individal responding to the challenge of the unknown.

And so it is with the free citizen. To be free a citizen has to know his or her rights and duties so that practical social cooperation is a possibility. A free citizen needs rules but he or she cannot be prescribed goals. That is why institutions such as the Spanish Inquisition or the Communist Party of the Soviet Union or the Central Intelligence Agency of the United States unrestrained by Congress are evil.

5   The Crisis of Capitalist Societies—Stage I

The economic order most likely to enable individuals to become free, self-sufficient, cooperative human beings responsible for and able to shape their own lives is the one to which we have given the name *laissez-faire* capitalism. It has never existed; it does not exist and there is only a small chance that it will ever exist outside the imagination. As much as socialism or communism, *laissez-faire* capitalism is an ideal whose principal use is to serve as a means of understanding and criticizing what exists. On the other hand, there has been a time in history, and that comparatively recently, when here and there in the world, socio-economic arrangements and practices did approximate to a *laissez-faire* economic order, with the astonishing consequences, which we have outlined, of a breakthrough to a new order of human capacity, creativity and growth.

In theory an economy based on free exchange defines and produces justice, equates efforts to rewards in accordance with social and individual needs, and is both expansive and stable. How far short has performance been from theory! But then, how far short has practice fallen of theory.

The British, perhaps, practised the principles of a *laissez-faire* market economy more consistently both in their domestic arrangements and in their international economic policies than any community during the years between the repeal of the Corn Laws in 1846 and the outbreak of World War I. It is said that the British organize their lives pragmatically without regard for theory. Maybe so today, but historically this proposition is nonsense. For nearly two centuries the British generated a great body of socio-economic theory, and they made their policies in accord with theory, often in a very pedantic and exacting way. Their policies were brilliantly successful in much the same way as landing a man on the moon is a result of applying consistently the theories of the physical sciences. It may be supposed not unreasonably that Britain has landed in the soup because the British have ceased generating consistent theories and have been guided by short-term, *ad hoc* pragmatism in response to the agitation of the ignorant in the pursuit of the unobtainable.

The Americans had a brief moment of theoretical consistency and insight when they first planned the policies of the United States and established their constitution, but thereafter freedom was defined in terms not of principle but of the absence of it, and not least in matters of economic organization. The one big and saving American decision was to create an area of free trade of continental dimensions, and this advantage was so great that it still operates to correct the idiocies and mistakes which arise from the greedy, short-sighted inconsistencies of special interests. The most notable breach of the principles of a free, competitive economy by the Americans was their persistent refusal to open their markets to the competition of the outside world. Never content with the great natural advantages they enjoyed of abundant resources, the industrial interests of the United States—and this embraced both employers and wage workers—wanted more advantages, with the result that many interests were obliged to accept the semi-monopolistic modification of market forces to their disadvantage.

In Europe the free market areas were never larger than the nation states. Germany, France and Austria-Hungary all practised policies of interference with international competition.

In another way there was massive interference with the

competitive bargaining process. This was in the matter of wage bargaining. In the United States in particular employers worked strenuously to impose their definition of a free labour market, i.e. a market in which there was perfect competition among individuals offering their services. Given the overall environment in the United States, the labour market was naturally free, and for many generations labour was a scarce commodity even under the slave regime where men and women were bought outright and were thus deprived of the right to sell their labour power to the best advantage of themselves. But there is nothing inconsistent with a free labour market for sellers of labour power to employ intermediary bargaining agents with specialist knowledge of bargaining techniques in order to achieve the best bargains for themselves. Employers and others employ specialists in law to do their legal business and technologists to solve technological problems. The trade unionist conceived of as a specialist in bargaining and not as an organizer of a monopoly is as much an indispensable feature of a free labour market as a futures dealer is an indispensable part of a free commodity market or a stockbroker of a free capital market. What happened in the United States was the emergence of small craft unions which were a stimulus rather than otherwise to monopolistic tendencies among industrial and transport interests and had the effect of prejudicing the interest of the participants in the labour market as a whole.

These massive defects of the free competitive market economy of the United States produced a social catastrophe of unprecedented severity measured in terms of decline in total productivity and the unemployment of the factors of production; land, labour and capital alike. The depression of the 1930s began in Europe in 1928, and hit the United States, the focal point of its intensity, in the autumn of 1929. For four years the economy was in acute disarray. Nearly 25 per cent of the work force were unemployed by 1932 and in the spring of 1933 the entire banking system closed. This was *the* crisis of the capitalist economy.

In order to suggest some of the factors in this crisis, let us consider the experience of Henry Ford and the Ford Motor Company. For two decades, from roughly 1910 to 1930, Henry Ford occupied an important place not only in the industrial and commercial life of the world but perhaps even more importantly in the imagination of people in the United States and elsewhere. The socialists, communists and other critics and enemies of capitalist free enterprise began to refer to Fordism and not capitalism as the object of their opposition. At times Ford regarded himself as a prophet of some significance. For example, he thought he could stop World War I, and organized a mission which he launched on Europe in the form of a 'peace ship'. This excursion into world politics, of course, failed, but at the level of the real material life of the American community Ford had a profound impact in two directions.

As an industrialist it was Henry Ford's conscious aim to 'put people on wheels', i.e. to produce a motor vehicle sufficiently low in price for every family in the United States and even in the world to possess one. This was a truly democratic objective of power for the people: the power to move distances and at speeds hitherto unimagined, and at the disposal of individuals in the way railways and steamships were not. When one considers that, in 1900, 50 per cent more people lived in rural America than lived in cities, the prospect of being able to escape from rural isolation power-fully affected the majority, and the similar possibility was no less appealing to the city dweller. The psychological con-sequences of the cheap motor vehicle have never been fully explored by political thinkers, although they are well known to anyone seriously concerned with the real business of living. Unless one has lived and worked in rural America in the circumstances which still existed half a century ago, one cannot grasp the importance of the cheap motor car as an agency of liberation more appealing than any political programme. It is not accidental that the great imaginative political propagandist Adolf Hitler planned a 'people's car', and that, had not the diabolic and traditional elements in his personality and in his society triumphed, Hitler, like Ford, might have put the European people on wheels twenty years before this actually began to happen.

But there was another dimension to Ford's thinking. He believed that the people must have incomes sufficient to buy his products. His policy, adopted in 1914, of a minimum wage of $5.00 a day in the Ford plants struck the imagination of society in an extraordinary way. Up to this point Ford had been a very average employer of labour. The bonuses his company distributed went to the top levels of management and skill. In 1914, however, he consciously adopted a 'high wages' policy which ran counter to the prevailing policies of employers.

It must be borne in mind that Ford launched his high wages policy at a time of depression. To raise wages and to cut the price of his products remained central to his policy from 1914 until 1931. Although his inclination to benignity and humanity in his policies towards his employees began to change in the late 1920s, Ford's tactics in the presence of the depression of 1929 were still to cut prices, raise wages and expand production. In 1930 he increased his share of the market, and fixed $7.00 a day as a minimum.

'I was never able to reduce the prices of automobiles until I could first increase wages,' he told the *New York Times* in May 1931. 'I would rather put ten men to work at $7.00 a day than employ twenty men at $3.50, because the $7.00 men would have a surplus to spend which would put other men to work, while the $3.50 men would be barely living. The higher the wage the greater the purchasing power and the wider the variety of work set in motion.' (Quoted in A. Nevins and F. E. Hill, *Ford, Expansion and Challenge, 1915–1933* (New York, 1957) p. 575.)

But Ford's policy failed. He was overwhelmed by the depression. People could not buy a sufficiency of cars at any price. By 1933 he differed not at all from other employers in that he was obliged to lay off men, cut wages, cut inventories and devote more resources to new products. And he began to fight the unions. Always an opponent of unions, he now became a viciously anti-union force under the influence of Harry Bennett, an ex-pugilist with the instincts of a bully and the morals of a gangster.

Meditation on the Ford experience serves to illuminate some of the factors which contributed to the great crises of free-enterprise capitalism during the 1930s. What does one make of Ford's wages policy? Wages in the Ford enterprise from 1914 onwards were not fixed by market forces, and were not the product of bargaining between Ford as an employer and the men and women selling him their labour. Of course, the labour market was free inasmuch as no one was obliged to work for the Ford Motor Company and the Ford Motor Company was not obliged to employ any particular individual or class of individuals. Ford's employment policies were not typical of his time. He not only paid wages above the going rates but he employed recent immigrants who had to be taught English, blacks and disabled people. Ford set himself against the great majority of American industrialists and he earned much hostility on account of his high wage policy, and about the only point on which he agreed with them was in his opposition to unions.

That Ford should have sought to deal by his own actions with what he saw as an inadequate capacity to consume the products of industry on the part of the mass of the people points to a general problem of the American economy of the 1920s, viz. low incomes of the working population in relation to the productive capacity of American industry. It is true that there was already a trend in the American economy towards 'increased employee compensation' as a percentage of the total income generated by productive activity, but it seems obvious that the trend was not strong enough to absorb the output of industries aimed, like Ford's was, at a mass consumer market. Indeed, several calculations of those trends show them to have been weak or very weak compared with the movement towards a greater proportion of 'employee compensation' which set in after 1933 and grew in strength until well after World War II. (*Historical Statistics of the United States* (Washington, 1961), p. 141, F 61–66.)

If the Ford experience suggests something about the so-called free labour market, it likewise throws some light on the capital market. In this matter of raising capital and distributing profits, Ford was equally untypical of his time. Part of his populist background involved suspicion and hatred of bankers and a determination to have nothing to do with the world of finance. The Ford Motor Company was founded in 1903 by twelve men who altogether held in their own names or the names of relatives 1,050 shares. These shares could not be sold without the consent of the shareholders as a body, and anyone wishing to sell was obliged to offer them first to other shareholders who could buy them at the price offered by other intending buyers. The best estimate indicates that the maximum sum invested in the Ford Motor Company in 1903 was $28,000. For a short time the firm borrowed money guaranteed by the shareholders, but this practice soon ceased. The mighty Ford business was self-financed out of surpluses over and above current costs of operation. Only a small proportion of the surplus was ever distributed as dividends, but even so the shareholders had received by the end of 1915, $56,000,000, all but $1,900,000 in cash. A school teacher, the sister of James Couzens, the business manager, invested $100 against the advice of her bank manager in 1903. When she sold her share some years later she received $355,000 on top of the dividends she had drawn. This happened in an enterprise the head of which was indifferent to money and profits except in so far as surpluses enabled him to realize other objectives such as producing the cheapest possible motor cars, making his enterprise independent of suppliers (a goal which prompted him to try growing his own rubber in Brazil) and developing into new fields like tractors. In some years he maintained cash reserves as high as $300,000,000.

All this throws some light on capital accumulation in the

United States. If Ford could do this without recourse to the assistance of financiers, what was possible for men who induced people to invest money in return for interest at 4, 5 or 6 per cent or got money from them by holding out the prospect of profits on shares? Little wonder then that a vast army of promoters sprang up more interested in producing profits than in producing goods and services, and even less wonder that eventually the expectations of investors could not be satisfied. Capital as an agency of production easily became divorced on a massive scale from its purpose as a man like Ford saw it, and became a mighty racket.

There was one aspect of Ford's experience which suggests that the free market did operate and had a significant and revolutionary effect. Ford was the first motor car manufacturer who conceived of a market for automobiles outside the limits of the rich and well-to-do who, in America and elsewhere, could afford to buy motor cars out of curiosity, for prestige purposes and for sport and amusement. He was free to gamble on this possibility and to produce a product which he could market on a mass scale. His success attracted others into the field, and competition had the effect at first of reducing prices and eventually of improving quality. Ford thought that in the Model T he had *the* motor car which the mass market wanted, and that the principal strategy was to cut down the selling price. By the late 1920s he was forced to improve comfort and performance and to develop new models. In this respect the consumers, expressing themselves through the market, were able to control and stimulate the producers.

Consumer sovereignty, however, was possible only so long as the consumer had the power to buy. When this power failed, as it began to do in 1929, Ford like other industrialists was hard hit. A wholly new situation had supervened. On the one hand an expectation of abundance, rendered something more than a politician's or a prophet's chimera by a brief moment of real experience, had been established in the minds of the people; on the other hand, the capacity to satisfy these expectations had become seriously insufficient.

This insufficiency arose, firstly, from the inequality of bargaining power in the labour market caused by the handicaps imposed by public powers on the development of specialist and cooperative techniques of bargaining among sellers of labour power, and the concomitant refusal of the public authorities to interfere with combinations of employers and the use of devices like blacklisting, propaganda and intimidation; and secondly, by the insufficiency of investment in tools and plant with the object of cutting costs, reducing prices and achieving a nearer equivalence of total product prices to consumers' incomes.

Establishing the causes of the breakdown and crisis in any economic system involves the identification of those elements in the system which are non-productive, i.e. those consumers who are not producers, who are parasites on the system. In the case of the economies of the ancient world and in any simple economy based predominantly on one or two kinds of activity such as agriculture or handicrafts, the identification is fairly easy: too large an army; too large or too luxurious a public administration; the sort of excesses which attract the invective of prophets and are susceptible to correction through purification and moral regeneration of a political or religious kind.

In a modern complex economy the identification of the parasites and the non-producers is much more difficult, and the modern economists have abandoned the concepts whose development might have enabled them to do so. The abandonment of the concept of rent, for example, has deprived observers of the means of identifying income that is not derived from work. The equating of anything which has a price with the products of work is the other side of the failure. In the matter of work there have been equally disastrous misconceptions, e.g. the description of any activity for which a wage is paid as a productive one.

The object of outlining the Ford experience in the United

States has been to contrast an autonomous industrial enterprise separated as far as Ford could separate it from the capital markets and from the system of capital 'accumulation' as it existed in the United States and in the capitalist world as a whole before the Great Depression of 1929. Ford demonstrated that he and his fellow shareholders could take huge profits—$56,000,000 in twelve years on an investment of $28,000 is a rather large rate of return. At the same time they re-invested in productive equipment even larger sums in the creation of an ongoing process of production which yielded lower prices to consumers and higher incomes to workers. A substantial part of the $56,000,000 of distributed dividends between 1903 and 1915 and even larger but undisclosed sums distributed between 1915 and 1929 were obviously not all spent on consumer goods. Neither Ford nor his family nor his fellow shareholders were devotees of conspicuous waste, and disdained to become Hearsts or Morgans or Vanderbilts. A proportion of what they took *out* of the Ford Motor Company must have gone into the larger capital of the surrounding society via banks, trust companies and the stock market.

But what happened to it? Ford devoted his main surplus to productive activity and its improvement. But did the surrounding society? Too often not. In the financial world sophisticated forms of robbery developed, and robbery by definition is a social activity by which one party takes the products of work or the money equivalent from another party at a zero rate of exchange. Producers of all kinds—wage workers and genuine capitalists—are vulnerable to financial fraud and deception just as much as the peasants and herdsmen of the ancient world were vulnerable to bandits, soldiers and governments.

The lineaments of events in the 1920s and 1930s in the capitalist world suggest two interrelated defects not *of* the market economy but *in* the market economy: (1) fraudulent and parasitic forms of capital accumulation, and (2) exploitation of workers of all kinds through obstructions to bargaining. The methods developed to overcome the consequences of these defects have established the principal elements in the present crisis of the 1970s.

At the very nadir of the crisis in the United States in 1933 when all the banks were closed and a quarter of the population were unemployed, F. D. Roosevelt took the oath of office as President of the United States. He was a skilful politician and a confused thinker. His first act was to declare to the world that 'we have nothing to fear but fear itself'. Brave words, but how to remove the fear?

Roosevelt's first instincts were quite sound. He sought to reintroduce some of the honesty which is the underlying moral necessity of a market economy. Unfortunately his ideas for re-establishing norms of social behaviour were as simple-minded as they were impractical. Workers and employers were to be brought together in syndicates stamped with the patriotic eagle of the United States, endorsed by the government and given the title of the National Recovery Administration. The NRA was a failure, but it contained the seeds of some saving reforms more in line with the requirements of the situation and more in keeping with the principles of a market economy.

These reforms were two in number: the Wagner Labor Relations Act and the legislation which set up the Securities Exchange Commission. The first piece of legislation had many defects, but it had one massive virtue inasmuch as it established on a national scale the practice of collective bargaining between employers and employees and ended the mythical proposition that the last man in a job queue is in an equal bargaining position to the General Motors Corporation.

The Securities Exchange Commission was based on the general proposition that anyone entering the capital market is entitled as an investor to real information about the activities and intentions of people seeking investment funds, and that the process of bargaining must conform to norms of behaviour that involve exchanging assets for assets or assets for entitlement to share in the outcome of real industrial and commercial activities. In short, it obliged financiers and business men to engage in real productive activities and not in schemes to relieve people of their assets in exchange for nothing. Of course, no legislation can forever protect people from crooks, but the effect of the legislation has been to force the more imaginative financiers and con men to operate outside the United States in the more 'liberal' parts of the capitalist world like Switzerland (for a time), Britain, Canada, Brazil and the little artificial 'islands of freedom' in the Caribbean.

The essential element in these two great reforms was the firmer establishment of contracting among individuals, their intermediaries and corporations as a means of determining rights, duties and modes of social cooperation among themselves. The state intruded into this bargaining about finance, production and the distribution of the products of economic activity to the extent that the Congress and the President of the United States made the rules for bargaining and appointed the overseers of the processes, but the state did not determine the outcome of the processes themselves. To this extent the market economy was strengthened and improved, not diminished.

These reforms had the effect of making more effective the market economy in the United States and this in turn had a number of advantageous effects in the rest of the world. But there were many consequences of the depression which weakened the market economy and created the set of conditions with which we are presently having to contend. Unless strongly and intelligently resisted, these conditions can mean the disappearance of individual freedom and a return to highly stratified and controlled societies bearing a strong resemblance to the empires of antiquity. The probability that this will happen is great. The belief of the Soviet leaders, for example, that theirs is the prototype for the future may not be fanciful. The operative word, however, is *may*, for if there is one truth in history it is this: there is nothing inevitable in society or in history. If men and women turn into slaves, it will be their own doing; and the opposite is equally the case.

The failure and near collapse of market capitalism in 1929 created a condition of despair and uncertainty among all kinds and conditions of people everywhere. This circumstance was the opportunity for prophets of every description. And why not? A deep instinct of self-preservation impelled men and women to consider alternative forms of social and economic organization. The reform and repair of market capitalism may have been the best road forward, but it was by no means the most attractive. Neither the moral ideas nor the organization of such a society are easy to understand, and the role of the state therein especially so. Too often the limited, liberal and open state, which provides the best political environment for an exchange economy, provides also the means by which economic interests seek to transcend and escape from the consequences of market relations and to gain special advantages for themselves. It is not, therefore, surprising that in open, democratic societies the interests of all those who suffered from the breakdown of market capitalism should soon attract the attention of politicians seeking office and power. Capitalists who had lost their capital, or who could find no profitable opportunities to employ what they had, were just as susceptible to the persuasion of politicians as the large numbers of wage workers who were wholly or partially unemployed. Those whose incomes had been reduced by the catastrophic fall in prices were under a like susceptibility, and even those with fixed incomes or stocks of liquid assets, who benefited from low prices, could find little satisfaction in an atmosphere of depression and general anxiety. It was in these circumstances that there developed the notion that governments have the duty to intervene in the economy, to plan it and to ensure its working to the advantage of all. The people who were most inclined to support state intervention came in the United States to be known, unaccountably, as liberals. In Europe, on

the other hand, the most ardent proponents of state intervention were more accurately known as socialists, communists
and fascists.

By whatever names they were known, the politicians who
advocated the use of state power to achieve economic
objectives had this in common: a strategy of seeking the
support of a significant proportion of the community in order
to control the machinery of the state on behalf of their
supporters. It would be a mistake to suppose that in liberal
states, of which the United States was the best and most
completely developed type, the state power had never been
used to the advantage of whatever interest happened at any
moment to control it, but both the theory and practice of the
liberal state always left open the possibility that no one
interest could permanently be served by controlling the state
and that market processes, no matter how distorted, determined the nature of production and the distribution of the
fruits thereof. The state itself in liberal societies did not
employ a significant proportion of the population nor did the
state provide incomes for them.

The American liberals and the European socialists, communists and fascists, however, developed a new conception of
the role of the state. They all assigned to the state a positive
part as a controller of the economy. Of course, they differed
widely about how this positive role should be played, and
equally in their tactical approaches about how to achieve
positive state control. Each tended to operate within the
cultural and historical contexts of their own communities, but
all had the same approach to state power in relation to the
economy. It is in this respect that all constitute a political
force leading man back to the hierarchical forms of society of
antiquity, and to forms of society more totalitarian than
anything known in the ancient world.

It is convenient for purposes of analysis to think of the
modern 'statists' not as a homogeneous group differing only
in names, but as a genus of which there are several species.
The American liberal, compared with the socialists, fascists

and communists, is unideological, pragmatic, little disposed to planning overall, and inclined to regard action in terms of advantage to particular groups rather than in terms of the economy as a whole. The European socialists bear some resemblance to American liberals in that they are pragmatic and committed to no sudden end of market capitalism, but they regard private property in the capital stock of society as an evil which must eventually be eliminated for moral as well as economic reasons. They are necessarily partisans of planning.

The fascists and communists do not differ in their belief in the necessity of total power in the hands of the state, and of mobilization of the people in a single party dedicated to generating positive enthusiasm for the state and to eliminating all those opposed to or insufficiently enthusiastic about the goals and behaviour of the party. The difference between them resides in their conception of tactics. The communists are the more radical inasmuch as they eliminate the capitalists as such in order to create a collectivist society. The fascists, on the other hand, pursued a tactic (and this is likely to happen again) of mobilizing all disappointed and discontented elements in market capitalist society in order to satisfy all aspirations within the framework of a dynamically planned expansionist economy. As compared with the communists the fascists were able to retain the organizational expertise of the employing and managerial classes, and thus were able to avoid the severe disorganization of production which was witnessed in Russia and more recently in Cuba. In terms, however, of creating a state-controlled, bureaucratized economy there is nothing to choose between the fascists and the communists, nor are the consequences for individual freedom any different.

The fascist species of collectivist is, for the time being, unimportant. The growth and development of this species as a response to the depression of the 1930s had, however, a powerful reciprocal effect upon the democratic world, particularly in the United States and western Europe. The threats of fascist expansion assisted powerfully in developing the role of the state in the western democracies and created the main problems with which the partisans of personal freedom have now to contend.

The present world crisis has arisen out of the growth of the state and its dominating role in economic life everywhere. This great failure now presents to the protagonist of an open, just and prosperous world the same opportunities for development along sane and humane lines as the failure of market capitalism in the 1930s did to the American liberals and European socialists, fascists and communists.

Put in the simplest way, the present crisis is the reverse of the crisis of the 1930s. Today there is a contradiction between the ability to consume and the ability to produce. At first utterance this proposition seems preposterous. Never has mankind produced more goods and services than at the present time. But it is the case that consumer demand runs so far ahead of productive capacity that in parts of the world poverty is increasing; in other parts consumer demand is so impairing capital accumulation and investment in productive equipment and processes that unemployment is growing. In one great industrial nation, the USSR, consumption by the state has been so voracious that famine would have seized the community had not nations like the United States and Canada been able to meet the deficiencies in Soviet food production and food inventories.

Governments and politicians are at the centre of this crisis, and particularly the governments of the advanced industrial states and the oil-producing nations like Saudi Arabia, Iran and Venezuela. They are the agencies by which consumption has been expanded beyond the capacity of the world to produce.

This imbalance between consumption and production has been achieved in three general ways. Firstly, vast expenditure of manpower and capital on the game of competitive international politics. Secondly the stimulation of consumer expectations and the satisfaction of them in the democratic states by auction politics and the implementation of their consequences. Thirdly the population explosion in the so-called Third World. Competition which can be organized as a beneficial regulating force in an economy has been stifled and in places eliminated, and competition has been powerfully developed in political life where it is at best wasteful and at worst lethal.

6 The Crisis of Capitalist Societies—Stage II

In a witty attack on corporate enterprise J. K. Galbraith once invited readers to imagine a circumstance in which an industrial giant, wishing to increase its turnover, decided to manufacture a commodity the production of which is technically feasible but which no one has hitherto wanted or even imagined he or she could want, i.e. an attractive little appliance for the production of monogrammed toast. This is a supposed example of contrived uselessness of which other real instances spring easily to mind. But Professor Galbraith has failed to generalize the proposition behind his wit. How does monogrammed toast compare with many items in the catalogue of useless goods and services imagined by politicians and servants of the state, brought into production, and paid for by taxation, borrowing or paper currency?

Once it was discovered during the depression of the 1930s that the spending of public funds could have a revitalizing effect upon the economy, and once this was explained by respectable intellectuals in terms which rendered scientific what a previous generation of economists and the public had regarded as reprehensible folly, the age of the public entrepreneur dawned, and we have never since looked back. In fairness to men like Lord Keynes and Major Douglas, whose thought provided a variety of apologetics on the subject of public expenditure as the road to salvation, it must be said that they, and particularly Lord Keynes, did not believe that an economy is a bottomless well from which substance can be indiscriminately and infinitely pumped. Keynes, for example, laboured long and successfully to bring into being a system of international currency control which served to compel governments to manage their financial affairs with some regard for the maintenance of productive effort equal in the long run to the demand for goods and services. He and his followers did, too, recommend to governments the practice of cyclical budgeting, a process designed to limit deficit financing to periods of slack economic activity, and to require in times of boom restraints in the form of tax increases, budgetary surpluses and the reduction of public debts.

Both of the restraints advocated by the Keynesians in the interests of economic sanity were adopted by the major economic powers outside the communist world. Both have gone down the drain. Why?

The economists cannot explain what has happened: Milton Friedman no more than Lord Kaldor. The explanation does not lie within the province of economics and particularly not within the province of technical economics designed to let computers tell us what is happening. If one puts garbage into a computer one gets garbage out, and this is the current state of play so far as economists and the economic crisis are concerned.

Pace Professor Galbraith, there is a difference between a device designed to deliver monogrammed toast marketed by a private corporation and a device, say, designed by the 'intelligence community' to listen to all the telephone conversations in Moscow. In terms of uselessness by any standard of reckoning there cannot be much to choose between one end product and the other. But one is bound to observe that the continual production of machines for the delivery of mono-grammed toast will depend upon the extent to which people do actually buy them. Not so in the case of recording the telephone conversations of Moscow even when they are sorted out by word recognition devices. No one can judge the

worth of this end product of technology in the service of
politics, and the waste involved is hard and slow to check.
And the cost is high. In 1971 the American people spent
$6.25 billion on 'intelligence collection'. One of the few men
who have had occasion to use the end product of the
intelligence community is ex-President Nixon, and he has
told us that the information supplied him was inaccurate and
false. Nixon may be mistaken, of course, but there seems to
be some consistency between what he has said and what
actually happened in places like Cuba and Vietnam.

The public entrepreneurs—the men and women who
invent projects financed out of public funds—are free agents
in the way that no entrepreneur in the private sector can be.
It is this freedom which is at the root of our present troubles.

Ah, yes, it will be argued, but public expenditure is
scrutinized and approved in a free society by the represen-
tatives who are elected by the people themselves. If $6.25
billion or other such sums are spent each year by the US
government on spying on other governments, this is the wish
of the American people. Some or all of this expenditure may
be crazy or wicked, but it is as much the responsibility of the
American people as it would be if a millionth of one per cent
of their resources went into producing monogrammed toast
machines in response to market demand. Where is the
difference?

In the first place the public entrepreneur—the politician,
soldier, bureaucrat, academic or whoever—devises his or her
project to meet an alleged social or public need; not to meet
individual personal needs which the individual may or may
not be able, or wish, to satisfy. Individuals can have views or
opinions about the activity of public entrepreneurs, but they
have no power personally to accept or reject the goods or
services the public entrepreneur provides. Any power they
have must be exercised politically in cooperation with others,
either by voting or by demonstrating or by attacking and
overthrowing the public authority. There is nothing specific a
member of the public can do, because the means of response

is never specific. In a market in the presence of a monogrammed toast machine one can say yes or no, and the yes has to
be matched by resources. This specificity is absent in the
public sector. The taxes which pay for the public service or
good are neither voluntary nor specifically tied to any good or
service.

This brings us to the second difference. The public
entrepreneur is financed by funds which are taken from
individuals by compulsion—ultimately, but not often, by
force. Theoretically and legally in Britain and in politically
similar communities there can be no taxation without
representation and without consent. But, again, there is
nothing specific in the connection between the tax paid and
the goods and services received or allegedly received. Taxes
are levied after a ritual of public consent and to some extent
they are still paid out of a sense of public duty. The growth
of a large body of tax advisers expert in interpreting tax law
and in securing the minimum payments by their clients
indicates, however, that the relationship between taxpayers
and governments is not much affected by either the ritual of
consent or the sense of individual duty. Taxes are that part of
the individual's income which he surrenders in the presence
of power.

This way of creating a pool of spending power is very
different from that which obtains in the private sector. There
the entrepreneurs or the established enterprise must seek
finance by an exchange of promises to pay interest and to
repay capital in return for immediately available spending
power, or they exchange entitlement to share the profits of
enterprise in return for immediately available spending
power. A specific relationship characterizes the investment of
capital or the lending of capital in the private sector. The
relationship involves an interaction of human judgments
concerning productive processes. For the parties to the
investment contract there is the prospect of both success and
failure, and success or failure is specific, defined and limited

by the working of the productive process itself, which has a measurable reality.

The way of the public entrepreneur or the authority in charge of an established public service or undertaking is very different from that to be observed in the private sector. The first requirement in the public sector is to establish in the mind of those capable of making decisions about public funds that some public benefit will be derived from the activity proposed. The areas of public benefit are specific enough, but benefits themselves are not susceptible to precise definition or measurement. This being so, the conceiving of benefits is an open-ended process. The public entrepreneur *may* conceive of benefits as material and specific as the needs which a private entrepreneur seeks to meet, and there is no reason in principle why a public entrepreneur cannot meet the needs which a private entrepreneur does. David Lilienthal, who played a major role in promoting and bringing into being the Tennessee Valley Authority, which produced electric power, reclaimed land and developed a variety of services to agriculture and industry, was as much a great entrepreneur as Henry Ford, but it does not follow that all public entrepreneurs need be of this character. Far from it. The public entrepreneur has before him the whole gamut of human fears and hopes on which to play. Indeed, his or her first need is to stimulate such hopes and fears in order to create a demand for what he or she plans to do. Once the demand is established and the organization is created to supply the demand, then an autonomous *raison d'être* for the enterprise comes into being: the need to pay those who supply the service.

Because no specific acts of exchange are involved in the provision of public services there is no way of determining what need is. Needs are invented and those who supply them find it very easy to persuade themselves of the need for their activity. Massive generalizations about desirability take the place of specific evidence of need. Education is, for example, believed to be 'a good thing'. It therefore follows that the more education there is, the more benefit accrues to the community. If education is a good thing, so is health. And so is safety at work. And so is security in old age. So is freedom from fear. So is freedom from want. And so on. We name it, and we can supply it. This is the tactic of the public entrepreneur.

Some public entrepreneurs appeal to the public at large in order to create a clientele and in order to drum up the public support which politicians up for election feel obliged to court. This was particularly true in the days before positive state action and large public expenditures were accepted features of life. Inquiries into poverty in Victorian Britain served to identify problems and to create a sentiment among the better-off in favour of some kind of action. What kind of action and by whom and whether interference in the lives of the poor was acceptable to the poor themselves were not so widely discussed. But the creation of a public opinion was necessary at a time when the presumption was that the state had a limited role in society.

This public identification of problems has some merit inasmuch as citizens themselves have an opportunity to judge the reality of the problems and the degree to which they are not imagined or based on third-party self-interest. But nowadays, when massive state action and state expenditure are part of the conventional practices of society, the public entrepreneurs need no longer publicly identify problems. Indeed, for success the public should not be made aware of what is prepared.

Let us take three examples in Britain of 'policy formation', as it is euphemistically called, which are enormously costly, involve the expansion of income opportunities and benefits to minorities, have no demonstrable connection with production of any kind and have been put into operation by Conservative politicians who are allegedly friendly to private enterprise, a market economy and individual freedom. These examples, all drawn from recent history, are: the indexing of public service pensions, the 'reform' of the administration of the National Health Service, and the 'reform' of local government.

None of these instances of 'policy formation' had any place in any political party manifesto. They all were passed through Parliament with little or no discussion, and no discussion of any serious kind in the media.

By definition pensioners do not work for their incomes, and yet a body of men and women numbering at least 1,000,000 in an economically active population of 23,000,000 have been put in a position of receiving increases in income equivalent to the rise in the real cost of living at a time when the working population of every kind and the investors of capital are experiencing a persistent and severe decline in real incomes. Compared with private sector pensioners, where incomes are derived from investment, the public sector pensioners enjoy enormous privileges conferred upon them by the state without any serious examination of this piece of 'policy formation'.

The 'reform' of the National Health Service has consisted of the creation of an administrative apparatus that is positively dysfunctional (a euphemism for useless or harmful). The proliferation of health service authorities of all kinds has vastly increased the political pork barrel out of which patronage is doled to supporters of the politicians. Much more serious from the point of view of cost and of the efficient working of the doctors and nurses, who actually do the work of attending the sick, there has been created a large army of administrators, managers, clerks and paper shufflers who absorb money as income, and resources in the form of office space, equipment and so on. In order to justify their activity of managing and administering they are obliged to interfere in the working of the hospitals, invent methods of controlling medical practices and destroy a profession made up of workers who really did govern themselves. Medical men have now a new reason in addition to low incomes for emigrating from Britain: the weight of administration imposed upon them and the destruction of their personal independence. The last stage of 'proletarianization' of doctors and nurses was accomplished under a Conservative government and a Minister who professed to believe in free enterprise. Under the Labour government, the British Medical Association adopted a strategy of 'industrial action'. Meanwhile,the hospitals have become increasingly overcrowded and dirty, the queues for attention longer, and the service to patients poorer and poorer.

In the case of the reorganization of local government, no significant body of taxpayers ever asked for it, nor did any body of consumers of local government services. The reorganization was dreamed up by a small body of public entrepreneurs who are still astonished at their 'success'. The bureaucracy in local government has been vastly enlarged by the creation of a third layer of local government. Thus, 'the span of responsibility' has been enlarged and this has been the means of justifying great increases in pay, the giving of golden handshakes to those disappointed in the promotion game, and the creation among the people who actually do the work of repairing roads, emptying dust bins and gardening in parks of a perfectly understandable demand for larger incomes, improved status, etc., etc. Between 1961 and 1973 the number employed in local government rose by 53 per cent. The total effect in terms of improvement of services to ratepayers has been on balance negative.

These are instances by no means unique of the higher corruption of democratic society. How has this corruption come about?

It has long been fashionable to deride self-interest, and a large school of moralists as old as religion have inveighed against its pursuit. And yet self-interest is a condition of life. A willingness to exert oneself to survive is one of the distinctions between a human being and a parasite. Even a parasite is sufficiently self-interested to sink its proboscis into another creature in order to draw its blood. Obviously so strong and so necessary an inclination has been considered by moralists concerned with how we can live together and cooperate for the common good. It is banal in the extreme to say that no man is an island, and that all are interdependent.

The problem is how to arrange human relations so that the self-interest of the individual, which is a healthy, life-giving instinct, can be made to serve the welfare of a whole society and all of mankind. Conflicts of individual and collective self-interest are destructive of individuals and baneful to society. This observation, too, is banal and obvious. A market economy is the only social invention so far in which individual self-interest can be expressed without ending in destruction. Alternative solutions of the problem all involve either direct repression or psychological conditioning designed to repress and extirpate self-interest. Castro's Cuba or the Trappist Order represent attempts at an alternative solution.

What is needed in our present circumstances is a candid look at the contemporary modes of expressing self-interest. We need to cut through the socialist, Christian democratic and communist cant on the subject in order to look at the forms of self-interest which have arisen as a result of abandoning the political, administrative and moral postulates and practices of liberal society based on a market economy.

It will suffice to take the example of Britain, the first European example of a community which organized itself as an open, liberal society based on a competitive market economy. From the revolution of 1688 onward the government was conducted within the terms of a contract made between the aristocracy organized as a political community in a Parliament and a sovereign authority in the persons of William and Mary. The Crown agreed to govern in accordance with the laws inherited from the past and made by the Parliament, and to finance itself from revenues granted by the Parliament for purposes prescribed by Parliament. The underlying approach to government by the aristocracy involved a recognition of the desirability of a general authority over the community, but yet an authority with limited and defined power. The predominant inclination was to regard that government best which governed least.

None the less, this government with the support of

Parliament addressed itself to the strengthening and the development of the conditions necessary for the functioning of a market economy. Essentially these conditions were: peace and order domestically and internationally; stability of the concept and practices defining property; and reliability of money as a means of exchange, a measure and store of value.

Surprisingly the first task of keeping the peace was executed by relying upon self-help and the mechanism of the market. Amateurs equipped with sufficient authority by the Crown preserved the peace and conducted the administration of local government in their own time and at their own expense. Internationally the peace was kept by an unambiguous policy of seeking to preserve a balance of power among Britain's immediate neighbours in Europe and of going to war if that balance was challenged or any British interest or opportunity abroad was threatened. The instruments for executing this policy were organized in accordance with market principles.

The British Army and Royal Navy were voluntary forces recruited by market means. Men were enlisted for payments, and paid while under the royal command. Victories brought bonuses paid out of the assets seized from the King's enemies. In the presence of deficiencies in the number of men, crimps were employed to round up recruits or money was spent abroad to rent men wholesale from European princes. The officers of the services bought their commissions, and these purchases were investments the profits on which depended upon pay, promotion, and victory, because all prizes taken from the King's enemies were divided according to rules which fixed rewards in accordance with soldierly responsibility, from admirals and generals to private soldiers and able seamen.

In addition to the rewards arising immediately out of victory Parliament sometimes paid cash bonuses to successful soldiers and sailors. The family of Lord Nelson, for example, received a grant of £100,000 a year in perpetuity.

This system of incentives, which related income to per-

formance, was consistent with military discipline and technical achievements. The soldiers who endured the harsh
discipline necessary to good organization and close tactical
control by officers and the officers themselves knew that
success depended upon both discipline and technical
excellence greater than that of any enemy they might encounter. If North America is not today a predominantly French
state this fact is not owing, as is popularly supposed, to the
enthusiastic capacity for improvisation of colonial militiamen,
but to the excellence of the Royal Artillery, then technically
the best in the world and developed, officered and manned by
soldiers who were not just patriotic, but personally motivated
to win victories. In a sense unintended by Edith Cavell they
could have said 'Patriotism is not enough'.

It is worth observing that once the bureaucrats and
reformers got their hands on the British state and eliminated
what they called corruption and purchase in the armed forces
of the Crown, British arms ceased to astonish the King's
enemies. A century of alleged corruption and purchase
witnessed Trafalgar, and the defeat of Napoleonic armies in
Spain and at Waterloo. A century of reforms which replaced
corruption and purchase with a meritocratic system of
selection and finally introduced forced enlistment ended in
Jutland, the Somme and Gallipoli.

The second foundation of a market system is a stable,
rational concept of property. The laws of England were
complex, hard to understand and required professional advice
for their working, but they had the great merit of certainty
and they were underpinned by a system of Common Law
which preserved the notion that every man and woman has
rights and duties which can be adjudicated or provided for in
legislation. Laws, too, were interpreted by a judiciary which
was by tradition and in practice independent of any interest
including the interest of the executive and legislative branches
of government.

As fundamental to a system of market economy as peace
and stability of property was a system of currency which

people could trust as a means of exchange in day-to-day transactions, and of holding assets whose exchange value did not erode. The government of William and Mary reformed and stabilized the currency in 1695, and the technical adviser of the government was Isaac Newton, the mathematician and physicist, whose genius established a new epoch in the natural sciences. On the base of stable money new institutions of public and private credit were developed which, until a time in living memory, could be trusted by everyone in Britain and elsewhere.

These necessary conditions for the operation of a free-enterprise economy were established by an aristocracy who as a social group did not depend for their incomes on government. Some individuals like Walpole, the Prime Minister for more than two decades, from 1721 to 1742, vastly increased their fortunes by holding office, but the aristocracy in general derived their incomes largely from rents and secondarily from investments in enterprise. Rent as a source of income depended on the prosperity and progress of the economy as a whole, and not upon day-to-day exchange transactions. Thus, the aristocracy, itself a mighty interest, was in the matter of governing disinterested and independent of government. It therefore had a capacity to govern in accordance with general principles and not in accordance with the demands and devices of little interest groups dependent upon salaries paid by the government and drawn from the produce of society.

Placemen and pensioners there were, just as there were salaried clerks in the service of government, but these did not dominate the government, nor were they a disproportionately large body of men in relation to the economically active part of the population.

The rapid growth of population and wealth brought about by a freely functioning competitive exchange economy created new social needs and new problems. There was no reason in principle why some of these problems should not be solved by state action. The characteristic solution of problems like, for example, sanitation, involved action by public authorities. There was in this no pedantic adherence to the principles of *laissez-faire*. The most systematic interpreter of the idea of enlightened self-interest, Jeremy Bentham, and the school of utilitarianism which grew up around him, were no enemies of state action. Indeed, they advocated legislation designed to achieve the greatest happiness of the greatest number. They gave an enormous impetus to the notion at the root of modern statism that enlightened social scientists advising governments can do for others what cannot be done by individuals themselves and that somehow it is possible to add up satisfactions and produce a favourable balance by legislative and executive action devoted directly to specific problems.

The expansion of state activities inevitably required a body of civil servants to perform the new tasks of government and to monitor performance. For many years civil servants were truly servants, i.e. persons acting under the authority of masters. They constituted a secondary layer of government below the policitians and were controlled by them. Just as it was the fate of the Merovingian monarchy to succumb to the servants in their palaces, so the civil servants in Britain have become the masters of the politicians. The old relationship which persisted at least until World War I is now but a memory expressed in the ironic references of modern civil servants to 'our masters'.

The growth in the power of the bureaucracy in Britain has its origins in the political process which was finally firmly established by the Revolution of 1688. The aristocratic government consolidated by that revolution was based on the idea of a contract, and expressed in the Bill of Rights and the coronation oaths of William and Mary. In contrast to the dominant forms of absolutism on the continent of Europe, the English and then the British government was open, and limited. There was no doubt about the sovereignty of the Crown, but the real activity of government was compartmentalized in executive, legislative, and judicial activity all carried on in the name of the sovereign, but carried on in practice separately in some respects and interdependently in others. The British constitution commanded admiration as a result of Britain's triumphs in war and economic growth and prosperity, but it defied easy description.

About one feature, however, there could be little doubt. The political process was competitive. We know that the political processes of the absolute monarchy were intensely competitive, but this was an intra-mural competition among courtiers. As a result of the Civil War and the Revolution of 1688, the British political process gave access to more elements in the community as a whole than any royal court could contain. Parliament itself was, for example, a court separate from the court of the king, but it was a power because Parliament controlled the financial resources which enabled the royal court to function and the active advisers of the sovereign to carry out their policies. Parliament in its turn was accessible to interests outside the government because the members of the House of Commons were elected in a complex, uneven and often curious way.

As a consequence of this extra-mural dimension of the British political process, the active part of the aristocracy—those who felt inclined to seek honour and prestige, or who were drawn to politics as the best of all games, superior to horse-racing or hunting, or those who sought to improve their fortunes—found themselves in a set of competitive circumstances in which advantage could be gained by appealing for support outside the narrow confines of the active political elite.

The inherent shortcomings of competitive, auction politics were not evident so long as it was believed that the business of government was limited, and that interference with the economy was positively harmful. Auction politics which yielded improvements in the market economy such as recognizing the right of wage workers to bargain collectively, which produced innovations in the making of contracts, which limited hours of work, which set and enforced standards of safety and honesty in economic dealings, and which opened the channels to honour and prestige to a wider range of the population, all of these developments did not undermine the essentials of the market economy. Changes of the description which owed much to political competition among the political elite often enabled the exchange economy to function more effectively and did not erode the duty and opportunity of individuals to look after themselves, nor did it protect the imprudent and the foolish from the consequences of ignorance, folly and inadequacy. It did not remove from society the natural discipline of real life, and it did not create a world of illusion. The existence and maintenance of the natural discipline of a market economy was not inconsistent with action prompted by common sense and humanity to take some care of those unequal to the hard facts of productive life, but when the action of the state began to be directed to saving those who had no grounds to claim the assistance of the state, then a course was set towards the circumstances in which we find ourselves today.

One of the most pervasive myths of the present day, entertained alike by Labour, Conservative and Liberal politicians, is that the growth of state action can be attributed to concern for the poor and what are called the under-privileged. Compared with other advanced industrial countries, wages in Britain are low, the social services are inadequate, the expectations of the people of all levels of income are unstable and uncertain. In fact the intrusions of the state into the economy have been in the main designed to protect the rich and the well-to-do from the failures—not of all of them—but of some of them. In 1890–1, for example, the firm of Baring Brothers was faced with bankruptcy as a result of the imprudent and excessive underwriting of investments in the Argentine Republic. Instead of permitting some salutary bankruptcies to purge the market of men whose judgment was not equal to their responsibilities, the Chancellor of the Exchequer, Viscount Goschen, made a secret agreement with the Governor of the Bank of England to underwrite with public funds an operation designed to prevent the bankruptcy of Barings. This was done without the knowledge of Parliament, and was as contrary to law and to the spirit of the laws as anything Charles I had ever done. The manoeuvre worked, and it was justified in the minds of the men who executed it by the argument that a financial panic was thus avoided. But we have to ask ourselves what kind of example was set, and whether it was not being established that if a firm is big enough and its mistakes are bad enough, then the state will step in to save it. What began as a furtive secret now flourishes for the whole world to see and to mock: British Leyland, the British Steel Corporation, the British Aircraft Corporation, the British etc.

The merit of a market economy is that it imposes its own discipline. This discipline is sometimes harsh, but the discipline must be equal for all. The Baring Crisis of 1890–1 revealed that this was not so, and it has been increasingly not so with the passage of time. The protection of failure and not the promotion of success has become too much the purpose of the state.

We now have a new manifestation of self-interest which has rendered inoperative the function of democratic government. Any expenditure can now be justified as a means of protecting a vested interest. The state employs so many directly and sustains so many who are not employed directly by the government, that no government no matter what its party complexion can prevail against the weight of vested interests dependent on the action of the state either to provide an income or to ensure an income. No political party can prevail against the combination of interests provided for directly or indirectly by the government.

These interests are predominantly consumers who are not producers. Firstly, there is the great army of pensioners. When pensions were funded and were related directly with past savings out of current income and the pensions paid were a return on investments in the productive capital stock of the community, the development of a system of pensions contributed to the expansion and maintenance of the productive equipment of society. Now public pensions are deferred income paid out of the public revenue—either revenue derived from taxation of the income and goods and services, or derived from public loans which absorb a proportion of the savings of the community, or paid in money printed by the government. No matter where the pensions come from or how much they represent a just charge upon society, they constitute a subtraction from the current income of the working population or from the capital stock of the community or both.

When one considers further that public pensions of all kinds are now index-linked to take account of rises in the cost of living, this involves in the present state of inflation much larger increases in the money incomes of public pensioners than in the incomes of those in the private sector. In the same week that the government refused to pay working policemen an income sufficient to cover all but a small part of the increase in the cost of living, the government undertook to pay pensioners the full amount of the increase in the cost of living plus an additional 1½ per cent increase in their real incomes. This indicates the strength of an income pressure group in a system of auction politics, and of the concern of politicians not to offend it!

Then there is the payment of public assistance of all kinds, and the vast army of clerks required to scrutinize the entitlement to public assistance. Whatever the justification for the payments, it must be acknowledged that the recipients are not producers in any shape or form. These payments, too, come out of the incomes and the capital stock, or potential capital stock, of the community.

Then there are the vast manpower-intensive activities of education, health, and local government administration which are to a considerable degree a necessary part of the apparatus of society, but the size and need for which cannot be tested; they are the work of public entrepreneurs and administrators whose incomes, prestige and opportunities for promotion depend upon growth and the invention of new 'needs'.

Then there are the publicly owned industries whose capital requirements and wages bills have to be provided by the government if their monopoly power to dictate prices is insufficient for them to break even or to accumulate their own capital.

Finally there are the traditional non-productive activities of government directed to keeping the peace and preserving the independence of the nation.

Taken together, all this involves the payment of millions of incomes, and there is no clear means of determining how much of this is a legitimate social cost which any economy anywhere would have to bear and how much of it represents payment for unnecessary activities (i.e. activities which few or no one wants) or straight inactivity much like that of the placemen against which eighteenth- and early nineteenth-century reformers inveighed so bitterly.

That so much waste and economic absurdity can exist in an advanced industrial society is explicable mainly in political terms. The state has the power to tax, to borrow and to print money or its equivalent in a variety of forms. This is a seemingly inexhaustible source of income, and the matter of dividing up this income is in the hands of the politicians and bureaucrats who have an ever-expanding clientele. Everyone wants an income. The capacity of men and women to invent excuses for paying incomes is infinite, and the clientèle they can recruit to justify those inventions is well-nigh inexhaustible, and in every level of society. In this matter the rich and well-to-do are no less gullible than the poor. Indeed, the well-to-do, particularly the academically educated, are better at finding places at the public feeding trough than the poor. The poor are the great excuse for public expenditure, but they are not its main beneficiaries. In fact, the poor who are not too proud to seek public assistance find it so hard to prove entitlement to their rights that hundreds of millions of pounds of benefits remain unclaimed. Not so the salaries of the civil servants hired to scrutinize them. The unions and confederations of educationalists, civil servants, business men and local government employees are united in crying for more, and they know how to get it.

As the burden of providing incomes for all these non-producers increases there naturally develops tension about who pays. It is easy to understand why there develops strong support for policies of wage restraint and the control of profits. A point has been reached and long since passed when it is not possible to find a sufficiency of real goods and services to provide real incomes for all the claims to income established by the state. The whole society finds itself in the same situation as the head of a family who weakly allows his home to become filled with idle children, lay-about cousins and free-loading friends. He may love them all, and they may be delightful people, intelligent, well-educated, amusing, affectionate and cultured, but the household will sooner or later sink under the weight of insufficient productive effort and insufficient income.

Policies of wage restraint and curbs on profits are means of keeping down real income and in some measure of limiting the burden on the productive system, but they do not constitute a solution. They are in the long run a means of exacerbating the problem. Producers need wages and profits in order to produce. Low wage rates in the productive sector force workers to seek overtime or second jobs, with the result that they are tired and inefficient. It is not accidental that British workers are both among the lowest paid in any advanced industrial society and the ones who work the longest hours. Equally profits are needed to improve the tools and techniques of industry, and to induce savings out of income in the society at large.

Because the politicians, regardless of party, cannot deal with the problem of non-productive incomes, because in every case they depend for electoral success upon the votes and support of the vast army of pensioners, public servants and subsidized industries, they cannot take any action, nor do they wish to take any action, to cut down the public sector. All they can suggest is wage restraint and profit control as a device to diminish the claims of the productive sector, and as a means of restraining the wage and salary demands of civil servants, teachers and employees in the public sector.

Taxation is a means of limiting real incomes, but this, too, does not solve the problem. Heavy taxation may be preferable to bankruptcy, but it is not a means of cutting down the size of the public sector and of the number of non-productive employments and claims to income which are totally unrelated to work, such as, for example, pensions. Effective taxation is in fact a constant temptation to expand the public sector.

Borrowing is a short-term expedient in fattening the public income. Of all expenditure it is the most insidious, because it involves expanding future claims on the income of the state while absorbing the savings of the community in the maintenance of the non-productive classes. The old British policy of reducing and repaying the national debt has long since been abandoned, and the British national debt is like a large hire-purchase account which enables society to take the waiting out of wanting but adds nothing to real income.

Finally there is inflation. Much nonsense is talked about inflation, especially by economists. Mankind has had plenty of experience of inflation, and there is no excuse, except the tendency of people to rationalize the avoidance of truth, for not understanding its causes. In simpler societies the causes were self-evident; the incapacity of governments to pay their way joined with the possession of power to cheat the people by debasing the metal content of the coinage and to increase the number of coins issued from the mint. The consequence was always a price rise, which in its turn was a means by which people with fixed incomes, or people with long contracts which fixed remuneration for a good or service, had their real incomes reduced and those with stocks of goods for ready sale profited from high prices. More often than not inflation ruined the societies which experienced it. Inflation contributed to the ruin of the late Roman Empire and Imperial Spain. Sometimes, however, it had the effect of stimulating the development of certain sectors of society by reducing the real burden of rent or long-term indebtedness, and by encouraging people to invest in productive enterprises capable of taking advantage of constant price increases. Whatever its consequences, inflation always had the effect of disturbing society and preparing the way for radical change.

Contemporary inflation has the same fundamental character as earlier inflation. It involves a debasement of the currency. The difference is that there are so many more forms of currency than there were in past ages, when metal coins and bills of exchange alone served as media of exchange. Nowadays a government lacking money because it cannot, or is afraid to, increase taxes and cannot borrow sufficient funds, turns on the printing press and issues IOUs on its treasury. The bales of paper and IOUs are regarded as the assets of the banks and they in turn lend to borrowers on the basis of cash reserves of government paper. Easy money and easy credit reduce the pressure on everyone to consider costs and budgets, and pretty soon everybody thinks they have never had it so good. Wage increases all round; booming profits; abundant public expenditure. For a short time.

A little inflation may be a stimulant, like a little gin in the system, but a lot of it has a transforming effect on society. The most obvious first consequence of increasing the supply of currency in order to cover the costs of government is a steep rise in prices and a fall in the real incomes of all those having contracts of employment which run for more than a few months. Very naturally this diminution of real income stimulates wage demands. Employers concede the demands and seek compensation in higher prices. Thus a spiral effect is produced. Government as a payer of income follows suit, and so the inflation roars ahead. At the point where any agency tries to stop the process—a government by cutting public expenditure or employers by refusing wage demands or by rationalizing their work force in order to cut per unit real costs—tension develops; strikes, demonstrations, political hostility.

The most damaging effect is upon savings. When the rate of inflation rises above the rate of interest or the rate of profit, saving becomes itself a form of taxation which can be roughly calculated by deducting the rate of return on capital from the rate of inflation. The volume of savings in some countries hit by inflation (Britain is an example) remains large for a time. This is due to social inertia, but inertia cannot long prevail over self-interest and rationality in economic matters. Short-term assets such as surpluses above current needs begin to go into real property and consumer durables, or are spent on consumer goods, entertainment and holidays on the principle of spend today because one's money won't be worth anything in the future. Thus, saving declines as a means of financing productive activity, and as this happens employers in the productive sector find it harder and harder to renew capital and to improve processes. A combination of increased money costs, industrial unrest over real wages, and general uncertainty prejudices the tempo of industry. Unemployment grows and this has a further reciprocal effect of discouraging investment.

In economic discussions of the present crisis there is a tendency to find the causes in particular areas or parts of the economy itself. There are, for example, the economists who attach an enormous importance to the money supply as a cause. It is a cause but not an explanation. Then there are those who attribute inflation to excessive wage demands which occur when labour is fully employed and a scarcity of labour develops. In this competition for labour employers put up prices to meet rising costs. This analysis leads to the conclusion that wages ought to be controlled, and for the sake of equity profits also ought to be controlled.

This last analysis requires some comment. If we can suppose a closed economy with no government or public sector, and no public expenditure, the employment of all factors will be in equilibrium. As employment reaches the point where no more workers are offering themselves for employment, employers will begin to seek to attract workers from other employers by paying higher wages, and so wages will generally rise. Employers will have to economize on wages by improving tools or methods of production, but the limit of this will be reached when the proportion of profits as compared with wages has fallen to the point where no further investment funds are available. At this point the demand for labour will slacken, the competition for workers will diminish and wages will fall. In a closed system there will be an equilibrium position around which employment of factors will fluctuate.

Of course, there are no closed economies and none without government sectors which draw off an increasing proportion of resources. Even so, the international economy bears some resemblance to a closed economy. Employers compensating for wage increases can only put their prices up to the point where they begin to lose out to competitors in other countries. So long as there are fixed exchange rates, the economy of one country will operate more or less like those of other countries, and wages and profits will fluctuate around equilibrium positions. If wages go beyond a certain point, profits will fall; if profits fall below a certain point and capital flow slackens, unemployment will develop and wages will decline.

In 1945 an international agreement to set up the International Monetary Fund was signed by the leading non-communist states, and by 1971 120 states had adhered to the agreement. The heart of this agreement was an under-taking to establish a system of fixed exchange rates tied to the US dollar which was itself tied to gold. The agreement had written into it provisions for flexibility, and nations having short-term unfavourable balances of payments could borrow from the fund to prevent severe declines in their exchange rates until their economies were put right. Of course, there was no authority which could force any state to maintain its exchange rates at the norms set by the Fund, but all agreed to do so out of self-interest and maintenance of what were regarded as free market economies.

It is a matter of historical fact that from 1945 onward the economies of the adherents to the International Monetary Fund developed rapidly—not all at the same rate and with the same degree of success, but overall the economic development of the world between 1945 and 1970 was unparalleled, and the advance in standards of living in all parts of the world—even the poorest—was remarkable judged by past experience.

Today fixed exchange rates are no more. The United States destroyed the system in 1972 and many of the advanced industrial states have let their currencies float free. Even in the Common Market countries there is less than agreement about the management of their currencies.

The reason for this is fairly simple. No government including the US government could face the implications of ten or more years of foolish, undisciplined public spending; of indiscriminately creating income opportunities unrelated to self-sustaining productive activity; of abandoning the last barrier against economic disorder, cyclical budgeting.

The world depression of the 1970s has been made by the governments of the great industrial nations, and not by the international oil cartel, the trade unions, the multinational corporations or any of the other figures of popular demonology.

Faced by a little burst of inflation in 1957, the British Chancellor of the Exchequer, Peter Thorneycroft, resolved to balance the British budget and to hold down and even cut public expenditure in order to preserve some sense of discipline. When the crunch came, the British Prime Minister refused to back his Chancellor; the Chancellor resigned. Macmillan was, of course, preparing for an election. 'You have never had it so good', he cried. He won his election.

The election of John F. Kennedy as President of the United States was, however, a stronger signal for the carnival to begin. By comparison with what was to follow, Kennedy was a modest master of ceremonies. He authorized a programme to put a man on the moon. As a means of spending public money, this project had an imaginative magnificence which many of the succeeding excuses for spending money lacked. Lyndon Johnson demonstrated how to carry Congress along with him on a tide of public money and he expanded the Vietnam war on credit. In Canada, Prime Minister Diefenbaker fired the Governor of the Bank of Canada and proceeded to drown his enemies in public money, and he made the bureaucrats learn to love him on account of his capacity to dream up the impossible in order to rationalize non-productive expenditure. Some governments held out, but by 1970 all but those of Germany and Japan had succumbed to the political arguments in favour of superabundant public expenditure. On the eve of disaster, the Japanese government was planning a euphoric splurge, but the political leaders were challenged and found out in time.

When the day of reckoning approached, Nixon and his Secretary of the Treasury, Connolly, wrecked the international monetary system in an effort to immunize the United States from the consequences of the debauch. Politicians who had learned nothing and forgotten nothing, like Pearson and Trudeau in Canada, Heath and Barber in Britain and Whitlam in Australia, continued to feed the flames. Harold Wilson, too, carried on the process and then quit.

Naming names does not, however, identify the political problems of the crisis. Wherever the auction process in politics prevails and people have the right to organize into political parties and interest groups, and then to vote, the victory of the spenders, the inventors of non-economic, non-productive jobs and the army of bureaucrats, is inevitable. As a result of sustained government intervention in the economy and the creation of regulatory planning and operative government industrial institutions, the number of people dependent for their incomes, prestige and promotion on the government-financed hierarchies has passed the critical size necessary to create a collectivist society. The end of market economies is now in sight.

For more than a century academic and militant socialists have been predicting the arrival of a collectivist, socialist order. Two schools of tacticians have developed among the socialists: the bit by bit school and the class struggle revolutionary school. These schools have never loved one another, but their goals are the same, and today the schools are coming together as they scent the possibility of victory and the final extinction of freedom and the market economy which alone can sustain it.

The revolutionary socialists have triumphed in non-capitalist societies where small numbers and dedication to assaults upon old-fashioned, agriculturally based hierarchies were positive advantages. In free capitalist societies like the United States, Canada, Australia, Britain and Argentina and in the bureaucratically controlled capitalist societies of western and central Europe, the bit by bit socialists have found a *locus operandi*. Today the bit by bit tactics are paying off, and even the revolutionary socialists in Italy, France and Spain are coming round to appreciate its value.

The major factor in the present circumstances favourable to the bit by bit socialists is inflation. This is destroying the popular basis of the market economy. Inflation makes it difficult and even impossible for workers, small business men and professional workers to accumulate the assets necessary to live independently at some stage of their lives, usually as they approach old age. The powerful force of self-interest is compelling more and more of the independent people to choose between attempting either the difficult or impossible through saving and investment, or the seemingly easy option of state employment, indexed pensions and publicly provided services in matters of health, education and recreation. Many managers in the private sector of British business are privately hoping and even working for the nationalization of their enterprises, not because their companies are failing, but because state enterprise looks more secure and holds out the prospect of indexed pensions.

This blindness is explicable. In the absence of moral education directed to understanding the nature of the public good and of one's personal responsibilities in this matter, there is a natural tendency for self-interest to generate narrow, short-term views of individual problems and prospects. Once moral education begins to assert that self-interest is itself wrong, self-interest becomes increasingly narrow and delusive and is more easily rationalized into something it is not. Self-interest never ceases but it can be corrupted, and is never more so than when dressed in the garments of benevolence, socialism and people's power. This is why private enterprise business men and industrial workers are able to cut their own throats on the way to the bank for government subsidies and paper money.

7 Bureaucratic Collectivism?

It will be evident from what has been said so far that the prospect of a collectivist socialist society and the elimination of a market exchange economy as a necessary condition of individual freedom has not come about as a result exclusively of socialist, communist and similar types of pressure and revolutionary activity. The bit by bit socialists and the revolutionary communists have contributed to our present condition, and the fascist experience, principally in Germany and Italy, had a powerful reciprocal effect before and during World War II; but the main responsibility for our present state rests with the avowed liberal and democratic politicians and bureaucrats and the solutions they have sought in the presence of the disorders and shortcomings in the market-exchange economy itself. The socialists and communists have, however, prophesied what is happening, and their doctrine of the historical inevitability of the process is a powerful element in reconciling opinion and conscience to present events. If one comes to believe something is inevitable, that something has a fair chance of happening.

But need it? There are no demonstrable laws of history, and every effort to establish such has so far come unstuck either through lack of convincing evidence or through critical scrutiny of underlying assumptions. What does emerge from the study of history is that men and women make themselves. There was nothing inevitable about the Protestant Reformation, for example. That happened because Martin Luther proclaimed that individuals could save themselves by personal faith in God and did not require the ministrations of a priestly elite. People responded to his assertion in a variety of ways and for a variety of reasons, but when a sufficient number did so the monopoly of the Church of Rome ceased. Equally there was nothing inevitable about the American Revolution, or any other revolution, least of all the Russian Revolution.

In our present circumstances we need only reject the notion that a collectivist society is inevitable. We are then in a moral and intellectual condition to think about alternatives.

The case for considering a competitive exchange economy rests on the evidence that such an economy yields benefits of personal freedom of choice, material abundance and self-development. There is something inherently objectionable and indeed loathsome in the notion that, once having become an adult, one will depend on others to shape one's life, and that only sportsmen, entertainers and artists are allowed to create their own lives out of their own achievements. That we can all be provided for by others from the womb to the tomb is not only disgusting, it is impractical.

The benefits of free market economies are evidenced in the history of communities where such economies have been allowed most to develop, and the benefits of freedom, abundance and personal self-confidence and creativity are least present where exchange economies have been most suppressed or altogether eliminated.

The obstacles to the restoration and perfection of exchange economies are political. Let us take the case of the United Kingdom, which today is the furthest advanced of any mature industrial community along the road to a totally collectivist condition.

In the United Kingdom the political drama is depicted as a contest between workers and capitalists. The workers are the good guys; the capitalists the bad guys. To maximize wages is good; to maximize profits is bad. The victory of the workers means freedom; the victory of the capitalists means fascism.

This crude scenario is based on the theory of the class struggle. During the last forty years the theory has become established in the United Kingdom as a social myth so widely and popularly disseminated that it informs the underlying intellectual assumptions of a wide spectrum of journalists of all kinds, intellectuals, academics both in and out of the social sciences, clerics and politicians. It is with no sense of shock that one can hear a TV journalist ask a question like: 'Don't you find it difficult to be a Christian and a business man?'; or a student say, 'I couldn't possibly think of going into business to make money'; or a bishop invite us to learn from the Soviet experience. Leaders of mineworkers like Arthur Scargill will foam with anger about the bosses and the profiteers even though there are no privately owned coal mines in Britain, and the miners' opportunity to make a living only exists because the British people provide them with the tools and organization to do so.

It would be bad enough if all this involved only a false morality. Worse, it provides the intellectual foundation of false economic analysis. The problem of inflation is depicted, for example, as one which arises either from the 'excessive' demands for wages on the part of workers or the 'excessive' seeking after profits by employers, or both. If this is so, and it is assumed to be so by those who accept the marxist-socialist analysis, it follows that the escape from inflation can be effected by controlling wages and profits and prices. This is, in fact, the policy pursued by all British governments. The emphasis varies, of course, but the policy is always essentially the same. And this is not surprising because controls mean more work and more power for the bureaucrats and politicians.

The political problem is to find a way out of this division in the ranks of the productive part of the community and to align the workers and employers into a solid body opposed to the non-productive elements dependent on incomes provided by the state. Such an alignment of productive elements has seldom been achieved in the history of British domestic politics. Here and there such an alignment has emerged over certain issues such as the repeal of the Corn Laws or regionally such as the unity of the producing interests in Birmingham and the Black Country from the eighteenth century until 1945.

The Birmingham experience is instructive, and suggests something of the prosperity, freedom from depression and adaptability which are possible when producers are aligned and not opposed politically. Birmingham was never cursed with a charter which lent the powers of the state to the entrenchment of vested interests. It flourished in the eighteenth and early nineteenth centuries as a truly free city where anyone could settle and could pursue any trade or business. It was a community distinguished for its intellectual enlightenment and the absence of religious and professional vested interests.

From the granting of a parliamentary franchise in 1832 until its political life became 'nationalized' in 1945, Birmingham tended to be a one-party community, at first radical liberal and then 'unionist' after Joseph Chamberlain led the Birmingham liberals out of the party of Gladstone into an alliance with the Conservatives. Birmingham politics were so atypical of Britain as a whole, that they attracted the attention of early political sociologists like Ostragorski. More important, though, was the continuous prosperity and adaptability of the community. Even during the depression of the 1930s Birmingham experienced difficulty for only a short time, and was a place of immigration from Wales, Scotland, Ireland and other parts of England. It was, furthermore, the scene of the few successful publicly owned enterprises in Britain: Birmingham people were the pioneers of 'gas and water' socialism which really worked and really produced increased wages for the workers, profits for the ratepayers and reduced prices for consumers. And this was largely because the local government was run by business men who knew how to manage and organize and not by a 'thin stream

of excellence' recruited from universities or by people
contemptuous of commercial and industrial skill.

The Birmingham experience has not, however, been
typical of British politics as a whole. So long as the governing
elite were committed to *laissez-faire* policies this did not
matter too much, but once popular auction politics became
well established as a means of selecting the personnel of the
policy-making part of government, the present alignment
became entrenched. There are some signs of a slight shift.
The reduction to the ranks of Wilson and Heath is a hopeful
portent. Some of the more intelligent bureaucrats are
beginning to acknowledge that they have made a mess of
things. But these are only signs.

The task of realignment is formidable. It is necessary to
face the fact that some of the present troubles, particularly
inflation, reinforce the evils of division among producers.
During the 1920s and 1930s the stabilization of the pound
sterling, to which both the Conservative and Labour leaders
attached first importance, had the effect of easing tension in
the community. Real wages improved steadily without
agitation or pressure from wage workers, and the number of
trade unionists diminished. There was, of course, a terrible
problem of unemployment in industries like coal mining and
heavy engineering, but these problems were technological in
origin and were not susceptible to solution by 'creating
demand'. Today, however, inflation which steadily erodes
real incomes has been a godsend to trade union leaders, for it
creates real problems for every wage worker no matter what
may be the technological advantages an industry may enjoy.
The erosion of real wages endows the sacred myths of the
class struggle with an undeserved meaning. This is grist to
the trade union mill, and particularly to that part of the
leadership which is more interested in revolutionary change
than in serving as expert bargaining agents in the labour
market. Trade union bureaucrats, as distinct from wage
workers, have a vested interest in inflation because it helps to
make credible their propaganda.

Experience offers little comfort in the matter of realigning producers in opposition to public expenditure. The heavy weight of the non-productive interests in the political process creates an enormous inertia in policy formation. Some experiences of this kind are quite frightening. Uruguay was, for example, a welfare state with a special emphasis on public ownership and generous pensions. For some reason Uruguay was inappropriately known as the Switzerland of South America. Whatever it was, the predominance of the non-productive interests, which ensured a long period of uninterrupted power for the Colorado Party, the people's party, ended in the disaster in which the Uruguayan people now find themselves. As the years passed, the economy was progressively unable to bear the weight of the non-productive population living on pensions or drawing incomes in the vastly over-manned public services. Balance of payments difficulties arose as consumption outpaced production. Import controls were imposed. Prices rose. Inflation developed rapidly. Pensioners had to go to work to supplement their pensions. The labour market became glutted and wages were low. The public services broke down. The Marxists blamed the multinational corporations and American imperialism. Urban guerrillas were organized. The police caught the guerrillas and the civil government let them escape. The armed forces took over. The Switzerland of South America is now an authoritarian community of poor people, impoverished by the sentimental stupidity of two generations of politicians more concerned to distribute wealth than to produce it.

Argentina, with a per capita wealth and standard of living comparable with that of Canada and Sweden in 1939, is now a poor country for the same reason and with less excuse than Uruguay. Juan Domingo Peron, who, in power or in exile, dominated Argentine politics for thirty years, managed to unite in his leadership, in his policies and in his ideas all the confusion, evil, sentimentality and intellectual wrong-headedness of social democracy, fascism and marxism. He infected both his supporters and his enemies with his mad economic policies so that even when he was overthrown the economic idiocies he perpetrated lived on as entrenched features of political and economic life. The Argentine experience is bound to make one pessimistic about any society which allows consumption to prevail over production as the political basis of economic policy.

It is, of course, said in tones of racial superiority and out of ignorance that what has happened in South America cannot happen here. Why not? The nature of the .British political process makes almost inevitable the destruction of the economic foundations of freedom. This is not because any one policy decision is incapable of cancellation or reversal, but because of incremental inertia. The whole process militates against any participant in the process thinking of the problem as a whole. The intellectual climate and the moral atmosphere are so much the product of self-interest divorced from productive and commercial activity that anyone, politician or intellectual, who thinks generally and thinks differently is almost bound to be considered an impractical crank or a fool. Changes in political leadership have ceased to mean substantial changes in policy even when changed leaders profess change. The Conservative administration elected in 1970, for example, gave the impression that a spirit and a policy of free enterprise might revive. In fact the Tory policies were in their general character and effect more like Labour policies than anything hitherto attempted by the Labour Party. The triumph of 'Selsdon man' consisted in a footling policy of charging for admission to museums and art galleries. The real 'achievements' of Mr Heath's administration were indexed pensions for public servants, an enormously expensive reorganization of local government, and the development of a costly administrative structure in the health service and in public education: all good for the bureaucracy and bad for everyone else.

Ironically enough, it has been within the Labour Party that a turn-around in policy-making of a kind has been achieved. In the spring of 1976 it looked very much as if the road along which Britain was travelling would come more and more to resemble that upon which Uruguay and Argentina had so long progressed. At this stage Sir Harold Wilson rendered the greatest service of his career. He resigned. Few would then have predicted that James Callaghan and his Chancellor would put a brake upon the Gadarene descent. But they did. They allowed the International Monetary Fund to prescribe a policy, and they applied their political skills to its implementation.

What serious British subjects have now to ask themselves is how long they can depend upon a chance combination of internationally generated economic wisdom and social democratic political skill to prevent the further growth of collectivism and enserfment. James Callaghan and Denis Healey are not immortal, and the procedures by which leaders are selected in the Labour Party do not guarantee that a 'Wilson–Kerensky' type of politician will not emerge to open the way for the destruction of pluralist society. This possibility is a real one. Furthermore, the British electoral system guarantees that a minority always rules and the rituals of election can just as easily legitimize a minority of avowed collectivists of the left as a minority of unavowed collectivists of the right.

For the believer in free enterprise, free exchange and genuine civic freedom of thought, word and deed, the prospect of a further entrenchment of the big, well-organized interest groups is frightening both on account of its consequences for the individual and on account of the real prospect of its coming about.

The three major interest groups with which the politicians thrown up by the present electoral system have to deal are the bureaucracy, the Confederation of British Industries and the Trades Union Congress. Of the three the bureaucracy is the most cohesive, the least exposed to public scrutiny, the most self-selective and the best located in the power structure to ensure its interest. The CBI and the TUC have the merit of being producers of goods and services, but they are antagonistic to one another in terms of their belief systems, in their rhetoric and to a lesser extent in their economic interests.

None of these major interest groups, separately or together, constitute a majority of the people. Far from it. If, however, the politicians and bureaucrats in their desire further to consolidate their power bring these opposing forces together and induce them to hammer out a common agreement the consequences for free enterprise and civic freedom are not pleasant to contemplate.

But it does not follow that what is a possibility will necessarily happen. The CBI does not represent and does not have the support of the whole business community of employers, managers and financiers. Nor does the TUC represent or command the support of all wage workers. Furthermore, the CBI and the TUC are not united within themselves in the goals they seek. Elements in both the CBI and the TUC have, for example, common ground in their advocacy of the closed shop as a means not merely of managing industrial relations but of protecting their own power in their respective organizations. But neither the business community nor the trade unions as a whole are sold on the closed shop. Quite apart from its shortcomings in terms of freedom and justice, the closed shop is inimical to the interest of many employers and trade union activists. More and more both sides of industry are beginning to see what many have long known, that compulsory unionism weakens the bargaining power of both employers and employees, creates pockets of privilege and impairs production.

There are, therefore, some hopeful signs to be discerned among the organized 'big interests' and among the productive elements in the community generally. The bureaucracy is the big problem and the big danger. Its interest and the economic foundations of its interest depend upon political power, and so does the recruitment of its clientele among all segments and strata of the community. The attractions of corporative collectivism exist among the productive elements in the community, but among the bureaucracy there can be no other objective than the acceleration of progress towards a corporate state dependent upon more and more control, more and more conditioning of people from the top down, more and more interference in the lives of individuals and more and more destruction of property rights.

The increase in bureaucratic power and control, so noticeable in Britain, is an international phenomenon. The Common Market, based upon the notion of creating in western Europe a large, competitive free trade area, has come under the domination of a vast bureaucracy increasingly independent of public political processes and devoted to the entrenchment of vested interest groups. Beyond the limits of the Common Market is the vast bureaucratic empire of the Soviet Union where the ideal of bureaucratic control has been achieved through the modernization and systematizing of the tsarist bureaucracy founded by Peter the Great. Looking westward we observe in the USA, Canada and Latin America an enormous proliferation of bureaucracy and the perfection of the political devices by which large clienteles are recruited and controlled. In the so-called Third World, often rich in resources and peopled by the poor and/or the primitive, bureaucratic development is the most noticeable of all 'developments'.

Bureaucracies everywhere learn from one another, and they buttress one another by opposing the weight of one against another. The military-scientific bureaucracies of the USA and the USSR could not exist independent of one another. This is but the most conspicuous example of a general state of affairs.

But the bureaucracies everywhere are in a condition of crisis. There is an acute discrepancy between the promises of governments and the capacity to carry them out. Real wages and real profits are falling, unemployment is growing. The only solution of the bureaucracies is to employ more and more resources building more and more ships, planes, arms, and public works which are not needed and cannot be used. When workers and managers need work less, they are obliged to work more, or what is even more objectionable to fritter away their time and energy in over-manned and under-used plants, railways and government offices.

Corporate statism, socialism, fascism and communism are the fate of mankind only if we will it so. But the future belongs to those who learn from the past and are capable of seeing what government is and what it means when there is too much of it; who see that government has turned into its opposite from its excess: an agency not of peace but of anarchy; not of abundance but of poverty; not of equality but of privilege; not of open community but of enclosed and secret power struggles.

8 Government and Society

Although governments everywhere are sustained by the mutually reinforcing agencies of faith and force, the faith factor involves, and indeed depends upon, a large measure of abstraction akin to religion. It requires a mental effort to penetrate this veil of faith and to grasp firmly the fact that governments, secretive as most of them may be, are identifiable men and women who make specific decisions about the lives, fortunes, well-being or ill-being of the people who live in the communities in which they exercise their power.

Part of the faith in government consists of the belief that the sovereign state (i.e. an institution having complete and final authority and power) is the means of achieving something which for want of a better word we call salvation. Salvation is not a precise word, and it can be given a great variety of particular meanings. However, its general meaning is clear enough: a condition which is more desirable than the one presently experienced; a transformation from a condition of limitation, frustration and confusion to one where there is no pain, wickedness, bafflement, hatred and so on.

Fortunately for human sanity there are some reservations about this faith in government, if not in the majority, at least among individuals and groups here and there in society. An attractive feature of the thought of one of the intellectual architects of modern nationalism, Rousseau, and of Lenin, the most brilliant of Marx's disciples, concerns the promise of the disappearance of government. 'Man is born free, and everywhere he is in chains' is the first sentence of the *Social Contract*, and the last sentence of *The State and Revolution* reads: 'The door will then be wide open for the transition from the first phase of Communist society to its higher phase, and along with it to the complete withering away of the state.'

So much for words. The democratic nation state and the totalitarian communist state are, as institutions, both in the dock charged with high crimes and misdemeanours. And they will be found not guilty. Whether they are as crude as a genocidal tribal tyranny or as subtle, sophisticated and incompetent as the British government, governments will go on, and we need to face this fact.

The anarchists, gentle or otherwise, have no case. Their indictment of governments deserves attention; their prescription none. For this reason. They refuse to accept the natural, inescapable fact that men and women must work in order to live, and that under this stern necessity they are always vulnerable to the inevitability of robbery or government or both.

This is the problem. The solution is to use government to abolish robbery; to domesticate and civilize government and to render it as far as possible harmless and beneficent. Government is the consequence of evil; everybody's evil. The anarchist conceives of government as the consequence of someone else's evil; not of theirs and ours. The anarchists make the same mistake as all revolutionaries do. They seek change, salvation, what you will, by blaming and thence removing other people. Hence the euphoria; hence the commotion; hence the slaughter and finally the tyranny.

In considering the problem of government we have to accept that no individual, no group, no party, no class, no caste, no race is of itself perfectly good or endowed with any special virtues or mission, nor must we suppose that any of them are entirely wicked, unprogressive or otherwise objectionable. Furthermore, we have to accept that no one and no body of men and women knows everything or can know everything. Information is incomplete, inexact and limited, and always has been, and as far as we can see, always will be. The volume of what is knowable is always greater than the capacity of any individual or group of individuals to know it all. The acquisition of knowledge is a continuous but not a terminable process. We need look no further than the natural sciences to see that this is so. We make a hideous and tragic mistake when, in the contemplation of man and society, we suppose that a defined body of men and women, such as a government, has or can acquire the information necessary to plan even a city, let alone a nation or the world at large.

This is not a doctrine of intellectual quietism and despair. Men and women have acquired a vast fund of information, and they have made much use of it. But this information has been and is acquired in little bits for specific purposes: to paint a picture; to build a sewerage system; to send a man to the moon and back; or to eradicate rodents and crime. Disparate little bits of information can be put together for particular purposes, and likewise particular skills. But to suppose that because a group of men could build and decorate St Paul's Cathedral and another group can design and build a Rolls-Royce motor car, that some other group of men and women can order whole societies, plan them, control them, and bring them to the kingdom of heaven is to contradict everything we know about knowledge and its acquisition. There is a sin called pride, and there is an unfashionable aphorism, that pride goeth before a fall. *Circumspice!*

If we conceive of government as an abstraction—and there is a common disposition to say 'the government ought to do this or that'—it is easy to attribute to the government capacities, responsibilities, knowledge and virtues beyond those one would expect of individuals or groups of individuals. In fact, governments are made up of men and women whose individual and collective knowledge and information are limited by their own capacities. Excluding the inevitability of their own self-interest and assuming them to be entirely disinterested, it is still impossible for a body of men and women calling themselves a government to do anything intelligent or workable beyond the limits of their information. To expect a government to do things beyond the capacity of its individual constituents to acquire information is unreasonable, and for a government to believe and to assert that it can do so is a fraud.

Government, like any human activity, requires specialized, specific knowledge and modes of behaviour. The specialization involved inevitably reduces the span of knowledge. For the same reason that producers cannot themselves ensure the order which they require for their work and thus cooperate among themselves, governments cannot acquire the information to do everything and control everything. Governments are as much susceptible to the laws and the consequences of the division of labour and the need for social cooperation as any other element in society. It follows inevitably that governments, to be effective as agencies of social cooperation, have to define and limit their role in the community. Otherwise governments are a source of confusion, disorder, and the other massive evils of which mankind has had such abundant experience during most of the twentieth century.

The need to limit the power of governments in the interest of liberty and peace is now universal. This need is as much common to the American, British, French and Soviet people as it is to people suffering under some insane African tyrant. Let us be clear. The possibility of total annihilation in a nuclear war is real. Such a catastrophe will be the work of governments, not of their subjects. The depression and the economic disorder of the 1970s are equally the work of governments and not of their subjects. The solution seems obvious and is difficult: to reduce and confine the power of governments.

In embarking on such a task we have the advantage of drawing on past experience. There are few governments in the world which are not organized in terms of public laws which we call constitutions. Even when the personnel of governments offend against the constitution upon which they base themselves, they still require some definition of their modes of proceeding if only to know how to transgress the rules in the interest of seizing and extending their power. The solution of the problem of limiting the power of governments lies within the area of constitutional law on the one hand and within the area of opinion formation on the other.

We know from experience that the development and growth of free market economies in Britain and America were attended by a parallel adoption of limited government. Limitations upon the powers of government were achieved by *ad hoc* contracts such as those between the Crown and Parliament which followed the accession of William and Mary to the throne of England and more generally in constitutions such as that of the United States.

The limitations on government in Britain established after the revolution of 1688 were directed principally to defining the relationship of the Crown, as chief executive and commander of the armed forces, with the Parliament. The Crown ceased to have absolute power as an executive, but the Crown in Parliament remained absolute *vis-à-vis* the subjects of the Crown. The Crown in Parliament is absolute. It can do anything provided the procedures prescribed by itself are followed and its legislation is obeyed. There are only two restraints upon the Crown in Parliament. These are the laws made by Parliament and open to amendment by Parliament, and public opinion expressed in elections, the timing and organization of which are in the hands of the government.

An absolute Parliament and a democratic process of election to the House of Commons are the main ingredients of auction politics. Parliament can do anything. There is therefore no limit to the promises which politicians can and indeed must make to attract a sufficiency of support to win elections. In these circumstances what is of immediate and sentimental appeal assumes an importance in the making of decisions which experience has persistently demonstrated to be pernicious. In the politicians the impulse to survive by preserving their basis of support is always at war with their understanding and common sense, except in the case of the growing number working for the destruction of what they call the 'power structure' and its replacement by something in line with their conception of revolutionary necessity.

In the process of auction politics the powerful forces of self-interest operate all in the same direction and at the expense of the producers' interest. In a free, competitive market economy the forces of self-interest operate against each other as in any bargaining process and so tend to produce balance, stability and decisions involving shared benefits. Not so in the process of auction politics. Here competition serves as an accelerator in the demand for resources to buy political support, and to increase the prestige and incomes of the participants. Ancillary to this is the multiplication of tasks for the civil service, a self-selected elite whose opportunities for promotion and claims to income increase with the increase of their work load.

How can this auction process in politics be brought to an end, and the purpose of Parliament be confined to making rules for society? Likewise, how can the purpose of the executive be limited to that of umpiring and enforcing the rules?

Because the entire process of auction politics depends upon the power to tax both directly by imposing statutory levies on income, on property and on economic transactions and indirectly by manipulating currency and credit, the solution lies in this area. If we take away from the Crown in Parliament the power to manipulate the currency and the credit system we shall at once remove a source of power and diminish the possibility of making promises which can only be carried out by robbing first some of us, then all of us. If we further restrict the power of the Crown in Parliament to levy taxes we will complete the cleansing of the Augean stables and deliver the politicians themselves from the temptation and opportunity to make promises of income and benefits which are not the product of real work as distinct from artificially created jobs. If we do to Parliament what Parliament did to the Crown in the late seventeenth century we will restore liberty in Britain and ensure its continuity until a new breed of rascals discover new means of exploiting producers.

The constitution of the United States was originally designed in an atmosphere ill-disposed to government as such. The authors of the constitution were bent on strengthening government, but they honestly believed it necessary to take account of the antipathy to government and to confine the powers of government to the essentials which they considered indispensable for the making of the general rules requisite for the effective functioning of a free society. As it was, the constitution was only ratified after the incorporation of amendments designed further to limit the powers of government.

Limited as the powers of government are under the constitution of the United States and subject as the powers of the Congress, the Executive and state governments are to the judgments of the Supreme Court, experience shows that the constitution of the United States needs further amendment to restrict the powers of government. Restriction is required in the same area as it is required in Britain and for the same reasons: to attenuate and, if possible, to eliminate the auction process with its massive pay-offs to those who support politicians competing in elections.

In order to take from government the power to manipulate the currency and credit there is one simple constitutional right which must be conferred on all citizens: the right to hold assets in the currency and credit instruments of their own choice with absolutely no restriction upon what that currency or those credit instruments may be. If the Swiss franc is regarded as a sound, stable currency or the Japanese yen or the Dutch florin or any currency whatsoever and is, in the opinion of an American citizen or a British subject, the currency in which he or she wishes to hold assets, then those so disposed must have an absolute right to do so. In this way the citizen will have the means of escaping from the follies of his own government and will accordingly diminish the possibility of its ever being foolish.

The second limitation on the power of government is directed to taxation and borrowing. Both the American and British governments must be rendered constitutionally incapable (1) of raising money by any form of taxation except taxes on the incomes of individuals and corporations, and (2) of contracting a public debt in excess of ten times the average annual government revenue decennially determined.

These two constitutional limitations upon the power of government will ensure that government is excluded from the 'management' of the economy, from the political determination of the incomes of individuals, corporations and groups, and from restricting the advantages of a worldwide division of labour. They will end the possibility of pay-off politics by removing or seriously reducing the means of paying off. The political process will remain democratic and will be concerned with the making of the rules of society and umpiring them. Above all there will be the inestimable advantages of confining the activity of governments to tasks which governments can perform and of preventing them from attempting to do what they demonstrably cannot.

There is a third constitutional limitation which must be imposed upon the British government: a prohibition on legislation which in any way exempts individuals or organizations from due process of law and from contractual obligations involving payment for goods and services.

The method of establishing limitations upon the power of government is simple and well established in the case of the United States. All that is required are two amendments of the constitution. The procedure for making these amendments is prescribed in the constitution and has been put into operation on several occasions in this century.

In the case of Britain the imposition of constitutional

limitations upon the activity of the Crown in Parliament is a complicated matter. The referendum on entry into the European Economic Community provides a useful pattern for action.

The people of the United Kingdom voting as a single constituency should be asked to approve or disapprove of five simple propositions: (1) concerning the right of the citizen to a free choice in the holding of property of any kind including foreign currency and foreign bank deposits; (2) concerning the limitation of the taxing power of the Crown in Parliament to direct taxes on the incomes of individuals and corporations; (3) concerning the prohibition of contracting total public debt exceeding ten times the average annual revenue of the government; (4) concerning the prohibition of legislation exempting individuals or organizations of any kind from the process of law and the obligations of contract; (5) concerning the assent of the people at large to the powers of the Crown in Parliament and to amendment thereof.

What is here proposed is an addition to the British political process, i.e. a process by which the community as a whole determines the way of life of the community by assent or dissent independently of government. In this way the monarch will know more precisely than is possible at present what kind of society she governs and what are the rules of the political process which it is her duty to monitor. No longer will the monarch be obliged to approve of every act of her Ministers and her Parliament, but will have some very general rules approved by her people by which she will be able as the final expression of public authority to scrutinize the activities and decisions of the politicians. She will then be a real sovereign and not as at present a means of clothing with the prestige of her name and dignity the decisions of politicians the cumulative consequences of which are too often disastrous or revolutionary or both.

Constitutional limitations on the power of governments of the kind proposed will restore to the governments of the United States and Great Britain the character which they had during the great creative periods of the British and American communities, and will further clarify the role and purpose of government in a way which is not present in the constitution of the United States and in the constitutional laws of Great Britain.

The proposal to limit the power of government and to strike from its hands the absolute power to tax and to alter the value of money will fix the purpose of government and impart a stability to the social order which nothing else can. Without absolute economic power, there can be no absolute political power.

Underlying the proposal so to limit the power of government is the concept of government as an umpire and the process of legislation as the making of rules. As things stand at present everywhere in the free world, except possibly in Germany and Japan, there is serious confusion about what we are doing when we govern or submit to government or seek to influence governments. Ends and means are mixed up in a hodge-podge.

Let us consider what we do in the matter of governing and being governed by examining the analogy of games. Games and sport are well understood by the mass of the people and they command interest everywhere as perhaps no other human activity does. Games and sports depend upon rules, and upon the activity of umpires or referees who interpret and enforce the rules. Both the participants and the spectators conceive of justice as the equal, disinterested and impartial observance of rules. So long as something approximating justice is maintained in the matter of rules, games and sports proceed successfully. But the distinctive character of games and sports of essential importance both to players and to spectators is the absence of control over results.

If we were to import into games and sports a concept of justice or social justice with respect to scores or results, we would make a nonsense of sports and games and destroy their character. If, for example, the Football Association, in response to an agitation by supporters of losing teams, were to resolve to do justice by decreeing that all clubs should win 21 games each season and lose 21 games the whole appeal of the game would be destroyed and so would every incentive of the participants to perfect their skill at football. To propose the application of concepts of social justice in sport and games is a preposterous nonsense.

And yet this is what is done in our real lives. Rules which produce justice in human relations are neglected or superseded by attempts to produce social justice: to control and to dictate the outcomes of activities.

This is a senseless enterprise. How can one define social justice? Medieval man wrestled with the concept of the just price. Five hundred years of debate and effort produced no definition. All they produced were obstacles to movement, choice and enterprise, and in the end it was acknowledged that justice in the matter of rewards is unattainable. The modern quest for social justice is equally a nonsense.

We have developed sports and games as a simulation of life, and they command a wide and profound interest from masses of men and women. But we are killing life itself by endeavours to control the outcomes of human activities. Now we have to return upon ourselves and ensure that life simulates sport and games, the outcome of which we do not control but the playing of which is life itself.

If we limit the power of governments to tax and to manipulate the value of money, governments will be unable to control the products of work and to determine politically the distribution of the products of work. The task of government—a difficult one and sufficient for any body of men and women—will be to make, adjudicate and enforce rules concerning the just exchange of the goods and services among their producers.

The failure of the old liberal society manifest in the great depression of the 1930s was due mainly to the inadequacy and injustice of the rules or absence of rules governing exchanges of goods and services, and beyond that to the immaturity of the constitutional and legal foundations of governments which allowed for the development of auction and pay-off politics. As a consequence of that depression some reforms were made, particularly in the United States, in an endeavour to make the rules more just and better adapted to the development of the industrial and financial system, but overall there has never been a systematic effort to reform the core communities of the free-enterprise world based upon the principles implicit in and necessary to a free-exchange economy.

The American economy will serve as an example of the inadequate, piecemeal nature of the endeavours at reform. The depression of the 1930s was caused on the economic side by a massive failure of demand. This had its origins in the inadequacy and the injustice of the rules governing exchanges between wage workers and the buyers of labour power, and the inadequacies of the rules governing capital transactions. Both these sources of evil were more or less put right by the legislation establishing the Securities Exchange Commission and the right nationally of wage workers to bargain collectively and to make contracts concerning the terms on which workers exchanged their labour power for wages. Unfortunately, however, the exigencies of the moment in trying to alleviate the consequences of the failure of the investment process produced the practice of using the power to tax and to manipulate currency and credit to finance both income and investment. War vastly reinforced this develop-ment, and war, preparations for war, and prestige projects in the international community have provided the continuing excuse for massive pump priming.

The process by which the United States was becoming a controlled hierarchical society in which political authority prevailed over productive activity reached its peak under Nixon. By reaching a *modus vivendi* with the other great authoritarian states and by developing their techniques of political control in the United States, Nixon brought the American community to the point of transformation into an antique authoritarian society. Whether President Carter can check this development and rediscover, strengthen and modernize a liberal rule-making process remains to be seen. So long as he has the temptations provided by unlimited taxing power and the capacity to manipulate the currency, and is inevitably geared into a system of pay-off politics, his chances of re-establishing a free society in the United States are small.

As for Britain, the case is much more difficult. The British never did shed the forms of a hierarchical society. Much that is attractive in British society has its origins in the aristocracy of the eighteenth century, particularly in the sphere of the arts, architecture, the preservation of rural beauty, sports and games and in enlightened tolerance and good manners. On the other hand, the aristocratic disposition to paternalism and the belief that the enlightened, intelligent and responsible part of society is small in numbers and confined to the aristocracy and those of whom it approves have seriously prejudiced the working and working out of those liberal principles which the aristocracy sponsored and implemented for intellectual and economic reasons. There is now in Britain an almost total confusion about the role of the state and the proper mode of proceeding to achieve a form of productive organization upon which the people of Britain can rely to pull their weight in the world and contribute to the welfare of mankind. The most recent manifestation of this aristocratic disposition to rely upon ownership rather than upon work and trade is the belief that North Sea Oil will solve all Britain's problems. Much worse than this is the long-standing bias in ideas of social reform, which puts a premium on doing things for the poor, the under-privileged (a word only privileged people could dream up) and all those not part of the top levels of society. Social reforms are conceived of as manipulating, controlling and providing for people, and hardly at all as making rules which enable people to provide for themselves in accordance with their own judgments of what they require and what effort they wish to put into meeting their needs.

The confusion of Britain is described as a mixed economy. A mixed-up economy would be a better description. Rules governing contracts between buyers and sellers of labour are non-existent. Rules governing capital transfers are an unprincipled confusion of highly technical meaninglessness which conceals fraud and failure on a gigantic scale. There is probably no failure of responsibility so serious and so little noticed as the unprotesting way in which large insurance companies, holding the savings of millions of people, and likewise the banks have cooperated with the government in debauching the currency and abusing the system of credit. Many opinions have been expressed of the English; even twenty-five years ago the phrase 'word of an Englishman' meant reliability in the matter of finance and trade. Not so any longer. Britain is a land of funny money, and no one can keep a financial promise because the medium of exchange is no longer a standard of value or a store of value.

9 Conclusion

The argument and the proposals of this book rest upon the general proposition that the present world economic crisis consists in a contradiction between the volume of claims to income and the ability of the productive forces to meet those claims. The expansion of the claims to income beyond the capacity of producers to supply them has been the work of governments everywhere and particularly the governments of the great industrial communities. While the crisis is affecting all states, its impact is uneven and two large industrial communities, West Germany and Japan, have revealed a capacity to cope with the crisis much better than the United States, Britain, France, Canada and Australia. Communist regimes have not escaped the crisis, but tight, repressive political controls have given to the crisis a different expression from that in less authoritarian societies. Like the fascist regimes of the 1920s and 1930s, the communist governments are able, for example, to absorb manpower into very large armed forces, a 'solution' no democratic government has yet had the folly or hardihood to attempt.

While the crisis is economic, its origins are political: the power of politicians working competitive political processes which involve recruiting support by the payment of economic benefits. The intrusion of this political factor into the economies of the world has blunted or removed the counter-vailing economic forces of markets, so that claims upon productive systems are unmatched by the activities of work, saving, investment and economizing in the use of resources. Because it is within the power of governments to recruit support without regard to the requirements of productive relations, all elements in society have learned to feed upon the public revenues. The rationale of state expenditure emphasizes benefit to the mass of the people and to the poorest in society, but the beneficiaries of state expenditure are not the poor or those who in terms of propaganda are called the working class. Indeed, wage workers are being obliged to bear the heaviest burden of the economic disorganization occasioned by heavy state expenditures. It is a sad and tragic fact that in the presence of these burdens the wage workers in many communities are responding to the agitation of those politicians who in their quest for power are determined to exacerbate the disease of state power rather than to limit it.

The solution of the crisis advocated in this book is a marked reduction in the power of states in their several communities. This seems a feasible solution in two important industrial communities: the United States and Britain. There are several reasons for supposing this.

In the first place Britain and the United States are communities with an historical experience of the beneficial effects of limited state power and of the stability and social peace which characterize liberal practices. In the United States in particular there is a traditional presumption against state power and state activity, and, in spite of massive state participation in the economy effected in the area of defence, there is comparatively little public ownership and direction of industrial enterprises. Furthermore, the American community has both the institutional means and the political experience of amending its constitution, and some of these amendments have been directed at defining and containing the power of governments.

In the second place the United States and British governments have had a large part in creating the political conditions for the success of the German and Japanese economies. The policies of the American and the British occupation forces in Germany after the defeat of Hitler and the German National Socialist Democratic Workers Party were directed to the elimination of the military and civil bureaucracy and to the institution of limited federal government. In Japan, the American policy was to break up the large landed estates, to require the institution of a democratic political process and to destroy the military and civil bureaucracy. Naturally neither the American nor the British government reformed their own institutions and practices in the beneficial way they did the German and Japanese, but none the less the results of intelligent policy are there to see and can now be applied to the conquerors themselves.

In the third place the United States and Britain together constitute an important segment of the world economy. What they do will have a powerful demonstration effect, particularly in Canada, Australia and New Zealand, and perhaps even in India and in South America. As it is at the moment, the United States and Britain are examples to no one, and their difficulties a source of *malaise* beyond their own boundaries.

At the centre of this disorganizing role in the world is their failure to preserve a stable system of currency capable of serving as a reliable medium of exchange, a stable measure of value and a trustworthy means of storing wealth. There is no hope of restoring the role of the pound sterling or the American dollar by the political processes now operative in the United States and Britain. Their economists can talk about the problem, but they cannot do anything about it.

It is for this reason that the people of the United States and Britain must take from their governments the monopoly power of defining, regulating and managing the currency. This is why the people must take unto themselves the right to hold assets in any currency of their choice. There are now 120 or more nation states in the world. A few of them are demonstrating their capacity to preserve their currencies as reliable and trustworthy money. The statistical possibility of two or three states doing this is rather good. If every American citizen and every British subject of the United Kingdom has the freedom to hold assets in the currency of their choice, the inclination of governments everywhere, including their own, to manage their currencies in a trustworthy fashion will be greatly strengthened. A severe limit will be placed upon the power of governments to rob their own citizens by the knowledge and the fact that their citizens have alternatives open to them and that they are not passive victims ripe for the picking.

It will, of course, be objected that limiting the taxing powers of governments will deprive them of the means of defending themselves from enemies; that we will fall victim of the Red or some other Menace for lack of the means to buy arms. The power to levy a tax on incomes and to contract a public debt up to ten times the annual revenue of a government will provide a sufficiency of money to finance any kind of defence requirement. Such a limitation will, however, restrain military enthusiasm, promote economy in this area of expense and oblige governments to conduct prudently other activities which are of a non-self-liquidating kind.

There is no reason why governments limited in their taxing capacity cannot undertake the provision of services to the citizens, provided, of course, these services pay for themselves. All services should be self-liquidating the same as privately provided services must necessarily be. The only exception should be provision made out of public funds for those persons handicapped by defects and accidents who demonstrably cannot provide for themselves in the way that the vast majority of people can. Even in this case care should be taken not to deprive handicapped people of their self-respect by providing them with doles. The handicapped are as entitled to opportunity and independence as anyone else.

The principal purpose and merit of severely limiting the taxing power of governments is to ensure as far as possible the generality of the principle of self-liquidation, i.e. that outputs at least equal inputs in any provision of goods and services. This applies equally to systems whose object is purely the provision of income as well as to those systems whose object is the production of goods and services as a means of acquiring income.

Let us consider this proposition as it applies to public service pensions. A pension is by definition a payment of an income to a person who is not producing, and a public service pension is a payment to a person who has not been a participant directly in the provision of economically measurable goods and services. Public service pensions can be provided as deferred income out of taxation. This is a simple and seemingly sensible way of proceeding. They can also be provided out of funds accumulated by investment in productive enterprises, and by this means be derived from profits of enterprise. No matter how derived, the pensions are deferred income. But there is a merit in the second method which is not at first apparent and which the first method lacks, i.e. a direct link with production itself and a guarantee against the danger present in all systems based on taxation that the productive foundations of the tax system will be overloaded and real income prejudiced.

The protection provided by indexing is illusory because the resort to indexing itself indicates that the productive base is not adequate to meet all claims. Indexing means that the beneficiaries of indexing are robbing those not so protected. The long-run consequences as distinct from the short-run advantages are disaster.

A further advantage of the second method of providing income for non-workers is that during their working lives the pensioners were providing annually a part of their incomes as investment funds. Deferred income provided out of taxation involves no contribution to production. Indeed, it involves a continuous and accelerating subtraction from production. Part of the present British problem is rooted in the maturing on a large scale of pension systems based on taxation and not on investment.

Pertinent as points like this may be, it would be a serious mistake to dwell too much upon them or even engage in debate about them. The most urgent problem of the moment is political, and it concerns the almost total ignorance of the very real possibility of the rapid transformation of our traditionally free, open market societies into collectivist 'social democracies'. If 'class alignments' in Britain, the United States, Canada *et al* answered to the description of the marxists, the possibility would be apparent and soluble. But there are no class alignments. Indeed, it is almost impossible to discern anything resembling classes where politics is concerned. Governments in the free societies have none of the characteristics or instrumentalities of agents of any class or group. They are laws unto themselves, and the agents of no one or no group except themselves. Their clienteles are large, but shifting and unstable. Like marauding bands of barbarians, the politicians act without principle because principles are too restricting. Anything goes, and so all goes to hell.

If we take only the examples of the United States and Britain it is possible to see why this condition of moral chaos has come about. Both societies have enjoyed great success: the United States as a productive, innovative and powerful society; Britain as an attractive civilization, now in many ways the cultural capital of the world. But the success has obscured the foundations of success and the rational principles from which success has sprung. The result is that what has happened is taken for granted. And not only taken for granted, but loved in and for itself. Anything concerned with principle which might seem to impair the enjoyment is disregarded and desperate efforts are always made to find compromises or ways out.

The spirit which sent Mr Chamberlain to Munich, which prompted what he did there and which won him the hysterical approval of the British population, is now the animating spirit of British society. Such a spirit is less present in the United States, but it is none the less a danger.

The most recent well-defined example of the spirit manifested itself in Britain in 1973–4. The crisis then was real, for all the chickens of fifteen years of irresponsible government spending were coming home to roost. There was a variety of ways in which the crisis could have been faced. The Prime Minister, Edward Heath, decided to face it as a determined resistance to the pressure and threats of a large and powerful vested interest: the miners and electricity workers. A three-day week in the interest of economizing energy resources was proclaimed. The TV was turned down, and so were the lights. A war-time austerity was prepared. Then an election was called. What happened?

The government began to run scared. The lights were turned up. Everyone made for the middle of the road: the Prime Minister, the Opposition, the communist leaders of the trade unions, everyone. A great sigh of relief went up. Things were not as bad as they had been made out to be. Labour won the election; or nearly so. The Liberals abdicated. The supreme opportunist of our time took office, and he deserved to do so. In his endless capacity for double talk Sir Harold Wilson exactly represented the spirit of the times: the spirit which says we have never had it so good; let us put off until tonorrow what should be done today.

The plain fact is that the existing political processes have exhausted their possibilities and are producing the opposite of what they were intended by their creators to achieve. A new process is required. This can be done, not by turning the clock back, but by resuming the development of liberal principles; by limiting the sovereignty of governments and by ensuring that on the economic plane a market organization is perfected and allowed to operate to the benefit of all.

It will at once be objected that the development of a *laissez-faire* economic order will enable the strong to devour the weak, the rich to grow richer and the large corporations to grow larger at the expense of small enterprises and the wage workers.

Experience shows that what happens in a free exchange

economy depends in a considerable measure upon the rules by which it operates and the moral understanding of those who make the rules and apply them. Free exchange in a complex industrial society with a sophisticated financial machinery for the allocation of capital resources and a well-organized system of bargaining in labour and commodity markets can only function on the basis of full and honest information available to all. Honesty is fundamentally a matter of moral sentiment, but as an operational principle in society it must be translated into laws having a particular character relating to specific areas of information and activity. We have many laws of this kind. We need more laws in some areas, and everywhere we need simpler, clearer laws firmly tied to the principles of the Common Law so that judges and arbitrators have more freedom to deal with particular instances than they do under statutory law.

Legislation which aims at establishing and defining what constitutes honesty and reliable information in particular circumstances is, thus, the first requirement of a free exchange economy. The second is the firm establishment of the presumption that any activity which restrains or interferes with the making of contracts for the free exchange of goods and/or services is illegal. The powers of the Monopolies Commission and similar agencies elsewhere must be greatly strengthened and extended so that strategies of individuals, corporations and interest groups aiming at advantages through limitation of freedom of exchange and freedom of enterprise are impaired and, if possible, eliminated.

The notion that the business of government is to protect the weak from the strong is so deeply ingrained in the minds of modern men that it is supposed that limited government will naturally and automatically expose wage workers, small business men and women and the self-employed to exploitation by groups possessing large stocks of capital. The supposition is, however, fallacious. The reduction of the demands of government on the market for capital will inevitably reduce rates of interest and force capitalists and investors to seek opportunities to put their capital to work in the production of saleable goods and services.

One of the most persistent myths of contemporary society concerns the supposed helplessness of wage workers in a free enterprise economy. Given just laws governing the making of contracts, wage workers are neither helpless nor lacking in initiative. In Victorian Britain wage workers with no help whatsoever from their alleged betters and often in the teeth of opposition from vested interests of shopkeepers were able to create the largest commercial enterprise in the country—the Cooperative Wholesale Society. Given an abundance of capital available at low rates of interest made possible by the reduction of government borrowing requirements, there is no reason at all why many new and more efficient businesses—some cooperatively owned, some privately owned—will not spring into being. This will mean real workers' participation and not the spurious, bureaucratic play-acting proposed by Lord Bullock.

The end of inflation by stripping the government of its power to manipulate the currency will have the effect of gearing prices to productivity and market forces. This will mean much greater stability of prices and expectations and more confidence in industrial investment. Gone will be the absurdity—completely rational and shrewd in circumstances of inflation—of railway unions investing their pension funds in art treasures. Art treasures are unproductive consumption goods which cannot possibly assist in the production of goods and services necessary to sustain pensioners. Art treasures are not productive in any economically meaningful sense, and they are only an asset on the assumption that there exist somewhere wealthy individuals or wealthy corporations or wealthy governments who will purchase them when funds are needed to pay Tom, Dick and Harry the wherewithal to meet their rent and to buy their meat and drink.

The limitation of governmental powers of taxation to income taxes will mean that the burden of taxes will fall upon the most parasitic form of income from property, viz. rents. Studies of the shifting and incidence of taxation in free exchange economies showed that progressive income taxes fell mainly on rentiers, and this was the original rationale of the progressive income tax. So it will be again.

We can reasonably expect that the re-creation of a free exchange economy will result in a more efficient and productive economy. This will open up the opportunity for all to make their own decisions concerning the level of their individual economic activity. Beyond a certain point, which varies with individual circumstances and character, people prefer leisure and non-economic satisfactions. This preference can only be expressed in a limited way in society as it is at present conducted. The burdens upon the producers of real goods and services are now so great that their real incomes are static or in decline on account of the demands of government for the sustenance of non-producers. If more people work in truly productive employments, and the need to work is more evenly and more justly distributed, this need to work will diminish for all. Individuals will thus be able to determine their own levels of effort.

A very probable consequence of a well-developed free exchange economy will be a diminution in the number of giant firms. Like governments, many of them are over-administered and crawling with parasitic bureaucrats. For their success they rely upon monopoly or oligopolistic positions often sustained by government handouts. There is something obviously corrupting and absurd about a set of circumstances which enables a large multinational firm of motor manufacturers to obtain over £100,000,000 of public money as an inducement to build an engine plant in the political home ground of a British prime minister while at the same time self-employed people are afflicted with Value Added Tax which costs more to collect than is mulcted from its victims. If the giant corporations were obliged at all times and in all places to finance themselves, many of them might very well begin to break up and so open the way for their better managers and workers to create for themselves new enterprises capable of doing better what the industrial dinosaurs do badly. For an example of this possibility we need look no further than British Leyland, a splendid illustration of the idiocy of unnatural growth fertilized by paper currency.

The most attractive feature of a *laissez-faire* economy is the creative challenge it offers to everyone. In such an economy self-interest is geared into social cooperation so that the maximizing of individual and corporate advantage depends upon the maximizers doing something for someone else, i.e. by exchange and not by fraud, intrigue or the resort to collectivist bullying and begging rationalized as social justice.

When the activity of governing is limited to the making of rules about human activities and ceases to be concerned with the outcome of activities, men and women will begin to enjoy something more closely approximating to democratic freedom, about which so much is said to so little effect. Society as a whole will have some prospect of survival if for no other reason than this: decentralized decision-making, a necessary and inevitable feature of a market economy, reduces the power and the possibility of political maniacs making irreversible mistakes. Mistakes there will be, of course; but the mistakes of a democratic, free-enterprise society are more like an itch or a fit of indigestion in the body politic than they are like a cancer or a heart arrest.

The argument of this essay is not against government as such. It is an argument, rather, for healthy government, which is stronger because it concentrates on what governments can do and is obliged to refrain from doing what they manifestly cannot. A lot of England, for example, is still a green and pleasant land. Free enterprise is not going to transform it into a desert of ugliness and utilitarian muck. The admirable rules governing the use of land and resources are not going to disappear, nor are the rules and regulations like the Clean Air Act which prevent public amenities from being destroyed for private advantage. What will cease, or at least be considerably reduced, will be the practice of solving problems of social and economic difference of interest by throwing money at them or by providing private interests with benefits at public expense.

Although giant industrial enterprises, both publicly and privately owned, command the centre of attention in Europe, America and elsewhere in the 'capitalist' world, it is still a fact that more goods and services are produced by small enterprises and by the self-employed than by the giant firms. These are the natural free enterprisers, for they have been created by and they live in a market economy. Limited government will enable them to come into their own because limited government means less interference and more opportunity; less privilege and more equality; less spurious social justice and more real justice; and above all a better correspondence between effort and reward.

Further Reading
Index

Further Reading

This essay is not based upon books but upon experience, reflection and instinct. There are, however, books having in various ways a bearing on the argument. Here are some of them, old and new:

Robert Bacon & Walter Eltis, *Britain's Economic Problem: Too Few Producers* (London, Macmillan, 1978)

Samuel Brittan, *The Economic Consequences of Democracy* (London, Temple Smith, 1977)

J. M. Buchanan, *The Limits of Liberty* (Chicago, University of Chicago Press, 1975)

Leslie Chapman, *Your Disobedient Servant* (Chatto & Windus, 1978)

David Friedman, *The Machinery of Freedom* (New York, Harper & Row, 1973)

David Galloway, *The Public Prodigals* (London, Temple Smith, 1976)

Lord Hailsham, *The Dilemma of Democracy* (London, Collins, 1978)

A. Hamilton, J. Jay & J. Madison, *The Federalist* (New York, Modern Library, n.d.)

James Harrington, *Oceana* (London, 1771; Heidelberg, 1924)

Stephen Haseler, *The Death of British Democracy* (London, Elek, 1976)

F. A. Hayek, *The Road to Serfdom* (London, Routledge, 1944 and 1976)

F. A. Hayek, *Law, Legislation and Liberty* (London, Routledge, Vol. I 1975, Vol. II 1976)

Thomas Hobbes, *Leviathan* (Oxford, Blackwell, n.d.)

Paul Johnson, *Enemies of Society* (London, Weidenfeld & Nicolson, 1977)

John Locke, *Two Treatises of Government* (Cambridge, CUP, 1967)

K. J. McDonald (ed), *Ouch!* (Toronto, Pocket Books, 1976)

J. S. Mill, *On Liberty* (Oxford, Blackwell, 1946)

C. L. de S. de Montesquieu, *Spirit of the Laws* (translated by T. Nugent, New York, 1949)

Allan Nevins & Frank Hill, *Ford, the Times, the Man, the Company* (New York, Scribner, 1954)

Robert Nozick, *Anarchy, State and Utopia* (Oxford, Blackwell, 1974)

A. T. Peacock & J. Wiseman, *The Growth of Public Expenditure* (London, Allen & Unwin, 1967)

Ayn Rand, *Capitalism: The Unknown Ideal* (New York, New American Library, 1966)

John Rawls, *A Theory of Justice* (Oxford, OUP, 1973)

Murray Rothbard, *For a New Liberty* (New York, Macmillan, 1973)

Lord Scarman, *English Law, the New Dimension* (London, Stevens, 1974)

Arthur Seldon, *Charge* (London, Temple Smith, 1977)

Adam Smith, *The Wealth of Nations* (London, Dent, 1933)

K. W. Watkins (ed), *In Defence of Freedom* (London, Cassell, 1978)

K. W. Watkins, *The Practice of Politics* (Nelson, 1978)

Index

American Revolution, 40–1
anarchism, 116
Argentina, 109–10
arms, armaments industry, 33
Attlee, C. R., 15
auction politics, 76, 90–1, 119–20

Baring Brothers, 91–2
Bennett, Henry, 65
Bentham, Jeremy, 89
Birmingham, 107–8
borrowing, government, 96, 122
Britain, United Kingdom
  bureaucracy in, 89, 111–12,
    112–13
  capitalism in, 34–5, 60–1
  government in, 82–4, 85–91,
    119, 122–4
  history of, 9–16, 39–40
  liberty in, 6–9
  'policy formation' in, 82–4
  present state of, 105–6, 110–
    13, 127–8, 130–1, 134–5
British Leyland, 139
bureaucracy, 4, 113–14
  in Britain, 89, 111–12, 112–13

CBI, 111–12

Callaghan, James, 111
Canada, 101
capital market, capital accumulation, 66–7, 69, 70–1
capitalism, free enterprise, free
  exchange economy, 50–1, 60,
  138–9
  based on exchanges, 53
  in Britain, 34–5, 60–1
  crisis of, *see* depression
  early development of, 34–7,
    51–2
  entrepreneurs a feature of, 52
  freedom and, 53–4
  moral and political aspects of,
    57–9
  in USA, 61, 62; *see also* Ford
  weak not exploited under, 135–7
  see also exchanges
Chamberlain, Joseph, 107
China, ancient, 23, 24–5, 32–3
civil service, 89
civilizations, ancient, 21–5, 33
class struggle, class alignments, 56,
  106, 108, 134
closed shop, 112
collectivism, collectivist society, ix,
  102, 104–5, 134; *see also*
  fascism; socialism; state
Common Law, 8, 87; *see also* laws
Common Market, 113